STUDIES IN GLOBAL ECONOMETRICS

## Advanced Studies in Theoretical and Applied Econometrics

**Volume 30**

---



*The titles published in this series are listed at the end of this volume.*

# STUDIES IN GLOBAL ECONOMETRICS

by

Henri Theil
*University of Florida*

in association with

Dongling Chen

Kenneth Clements

and

Charles Moss

KLUWER ACADEMIC PUBLISHERS
DORDRECHT / BOSTON / LONDON

Library of Congress Cataloging-in-Publication Data

Theil, Henri.
Studies in global econometrics / by Henri Theil.
p. cm. -- (Advanced studies in theoretical and applied econometrics ; v. 30)
Includes bibliographical references and index.
ISBN 0-7923-3660-7 (hardbound)
1. Econometric models. 2. Purchasing power parity--Econometric models. 3. Gross domestic product--Econometric models. 4. Consumption (Economics)--Econometric models. 5. Demand functions (Economic theory) I. Title. II. Series.
HB141.T5 1996
330'.01'5195--dc20 95-23666

ISBN 0-7923-3660-7

Published by Kluwer Academic Publishers,
P.O. Box 17, 3300 AA Dordrecht, The Netherlands.

Kluwer Academic Publishers incorporates
the publishing programmes of
D. Reidel, Martinus Nijhoff, Dr W. Junk and MTP Press.

Sold and distributed in the U.S.A. and Canada
by Kluwer Academic Publishers,
101 Philip Drive, Norwell, MA 02061, U.S.A.

In all other countries, sold and distributed
by Kluwer Academic Publishers Group,
P.O. Box 322, 3300 AH Dordrecht, The Netherlands.

*Printed on acid-free paper*



Printed in the Netherlands

# Contents

# List of tables

CHAPTER 2



CHAPTER 3



CHAPTER 4

CHAPTER 5



CHAPTER 6



CHAPTER 7

# List of figures

CHAPTER 2



CHAPTER 3

CHAPTER 1

# Introduction

HENRI THEIL

This book is a collection of essays on the use of cross-country data based on purchasing power parties. The two major applications are the development over time of per capita gross domestic products (including that of their inequalities among countries and regions) and the fitting of cross-country demand equations for broad groups of consumer goods. The present introductory chapter provides some of the highlights of these developments in relation to my careers in the Netherlands, Chicago, and Florida.

## The early 1950s

Consumer demand attracted my attention at an early stage. One example is my dissertation at the University of Amsterdam (Theil 1951), which was theoretical; another is an article on the measurement of the quality of consumption (Theil 1952), which was largely empirical. I have always found this theoretical-empirical combination attractive; I have some disdain for purely theoretical work in which numbers occur only as subscripts to algebraic symbols.

My earliest work on international inequalities was my inaugural address at the Netherlands School of Economics in Rotterdam (Theil 1953b; for an English translation see Theil 1960). This work was stimulated by my visit to India in the first few months of 1953. I found India's poverty very depressing. My youthful enthusiasm convinced me to devote my inaugural address to that problem and its solution. I could use the data from United Nations Statistics (1950), but I should emphasize here that such data (based on exchange rates) tend to overestimate the poverty of poor nations.

The two previous paragraphs summarize the beginnings of my work in consumer demand and international income inequality, but it is perhaps appropriate to add that these were only part of my research activities in that period. During the late 1940s and early 1950s I had a research assistantship under Professor David van Dantzig at the Mathematical Center in Amsterdam, which led to a three-part article on distribution-free regression analysis (Theil

1950). Other examples are two-stage least squares (Theil 1953a) and my book on linear aggregation (Theil 1954). However, I will confine myself mainly to the two topics of consumer demand and international inequality in the remainder of this chapter.

## The next twenty-five years

In 1952 I joined the staff of the Central Planning Bureau in The Hague, which led to my second book, *Economic Forecasts and Policy* (1958; 2nd ed. 1961; see also Theil 1990). In the next year I joined the Faculty of the Netherlands School of Economics on a part-time basis, and full-time in 1956.

My interest in international inequalities continued, particularly after I found two measures of income inequality based on concepts of statistical information theory (Theil 1967). One of these two measures is used in Section 2.2 of Chapter 2 of this book. Foster (1983) provided an axiomatic justification of these measures; see also Bourguignon (1979), Cowell and Kuga (1981), and Shorrocks (1980). In Theil (1967) there is an application to data on 54 countries collected by Dosser and Peacock (1964) for three years. For the first two years (1949 and 1957) these data have the character of estimates of past realizations; for the third year (1976) the data are conditional forecasts under the assumption that the developed countries are willing and able to provide all the economic aid which less-developed countries can absorb. My interest in this topic continued after I moved to the University of Chicago in the mid-1960s: Theil and Friedman (1973) used data on 133 countries collected by Hagen and Hawrylshyn (1969).

Consumer demand became the topic of major interest for Anton Barten, who joined me at the Econometric Institute in Rotterdam in the latter half of the 1950s. His article in *Econometrica* (Barten 1964) was an important starting point, particularly the Fundamental Matrix Equation. In 1965 I modified this approach slightly (Theil 1965), which led to what has become known as the Rotterdam Model for the system-wide approach to consumer demand equations. My two-volume monograph (1975, 1976) extended this approach considerably, while Theil and Laitinen (1979) were the first to apply maximum likelihood to the estimation of nonlinear versions of the Rotterdam model. I should also mention Barnett's (1981) book on consumer demand and labor supply.

Subsequent extensions include the differential approach to consumer demand, which allows the coefficients to be variable rather than constant. Other extensions include the demand for inputs of the single-product firm (Theil 1977) and the supply of outputs and the demand for inputs of the multiproduct firm (Laitinen and Theil 1978; Laitinen 1980); see also Theil (1980a,b).

The increased capacity of computers played a role as well. Laitinen (1978) raised the question of why demand homogenity is so often rejected. His analysis, which is partly based on simulations, showed clearly that these rejections are largely erroneous and based on misleading asymptotic tests. Similar results were obtained by Meisner (1979) for the rejections of Slutsky symmetry. These two papers are briefly summarized in Section 3 of Chapter 4 of this book. I continued to stimulate work based on simulations after I moved to the University of Florida in 1981.

## The most recent fifteen years

An important change occurred in the late 1970s when I obtained the data which Irving Kravis and his colleagues at the University of Pennsylvania had collected for their International Comparison Program. These data, based on purchasing power parties rather than exchange rates, enabled me to assess international inequalities more accurately. Also, they presented me with sizeable variations of real income and relative prices in cross-country demand equations. Of course, there is the possibility that such equation systems have limited validity because of different tastes in different countries, but the proof of the pudding is in the eating.

Considering matters of inequality first, I analyzed world income inequality in 1979 and international inequality (which disregards the inequality within countries) in 1989. The regional grouping of countries is by latitude: the Northern temperate zone, several tropical and subtropical zones in the middle, and the Southern temperate zone. In 1994 Theil and Seale published an article based on seven regions, honoring the memory of Jan Tinbergen, in *De Economist.* A second article in the same journal was published in 1995 by Theil and Chen, honoring the memory of Pieter Hennipman of the University of Amsterdam. These two articles have been combined in Chapter 2 of this book (with some additional computations reported in the Appendix to that chapter). Chapter 3 uses the same data for an exploration in spatial autocorrelation.

The first attempt to use these data for cross-country demand was made by Clements and Theil (1979), using pairwise comparisons of countries. That paper was never published; it appears here as the last chapter of this book. The pairwise comparisons were replaced by a different approach in Theil, Suhm and Meisner (1980); see also the monograph by Theil and Suhm (1981). Further modifications followed in another monograph by Theil, Chung and Seale (1989). This model, which is now known as the Florida Model for cross-country demand analysis, has the following features:

(1) The dependent variable is the per capita budget share of good $i$ in country $c$; the independent variables are per capita total consumption (in real terms) and the relative prices of all $n$ goods. The model consists of three terms: one for total consumption and two for relative prices.

(2) The real-income (total consumption) term is linear in the parameters. it is based on Working's (1943) model, which describes budget shares as linear functions of the logarithm of total consumption expenditure.

(3) One of the two price terms is quadratic in the parameters; the other is cubic. The cubic term is the substitution term, which is derived under the simplifying assumption of preference independence ("additive utility").

(4) The model is fitted by means of international comparison data for 1970, 1975 and 1980. It is not assumed that the error terms for any given country are independent over time. Rather, a first-order autoregressive scheme is used for these errors in order to take account of persistent differences in tastes across countries.

Chapter 4 of this book deals with the estimation and the measurement of fit of the Florida Model. The estimation procedures considered are maximum likelihood and a rival method based on statistical information theory. The latter procedure appears to be preferable, particularly when the sample is small but the number of goods ($n$) is not.

Chapter 5 deals with the cross-country variation of real income and relative prices, and Chapter 6 with the measurement of the quality of consumption. The latter topic serves as an introduction to some of the developments in Chapter 7.

## Concluding remarks

It might seem appropriate to end this Introduction with a tribute to all those who contribute to my work: teachers, colleagues, students, and visitors with whom I collaborated in the Netherlands, Chicago, and Florida. However, that number of persons is very large, and an attempt to make such a tribute would therefore be counterproductive. So I prefer to introduce the co-authors of the chapters which follow.

Kenneth W. Clements was Assistant Professor of Economics and International Business at the University of Chicago's Graduate School of Business at the time when he and I collaborated for the paper which is Chapter 7 of this book. He is now Professor of Economics and Director of the Economic Research Centre at the University of Western Australia. He spent the Autumn of 1984 with me as McKethan-Matherly Research Fellow at the University of Florida.

Dongling Chen obtained his Ph.D. in Economics at the University of Western Australia, after which he accepted a Postdoctoral Fellowship at the University of Chicago in 1993–1994. In the next academic year he was a Postdoctoral Fellow at the University of Florida. He returned to China in the summer of 1995.

Charles B. Moss obtained his Ph.D. in Agricultural Economics at Purdue University. Thereafter he moved to the University of Florida, where he is now Associate Professor of Food and Resource Economics. From 1991 to 1994 he was also a McKethan-Matherly Research Fellow at the University of Florida.

## References


Barnett, W.A. (1981). *Consumer Demand and Labor Supply*. Amsterdam and New York: North-Holland Publishing Company.

Barten, A.P. (1964). "Consumer demand functions under conditions of almost additive preferences." *Econometrica* 32: 1–38.

Bourguignon, F. (1979). "Decomposable income inequality measures." *Econometrica* 47: 901–920.

Clements, K.W. and Theil, H. (1979). "A cross-country analysis of consumption patterns." Report 7924 of the Center for Mathematical Studies in Business and Economics, The University of Chicago.

Cowell, F.A. and Kuga, K. (1981). "Additivity and the entropy concept: An axiomatic approach to inequality measurement." *Journal of Economic Theory* 25: 131–143.

Dosser, D. and Peacock, A.T. (1964). "The international distribution of income with 'maximum' aid." *Review of Economics and Statistics* 46: 432–434.

Foster, J.E. (1983). "An axiomatic characterization of the Theil measure of income inequality." *Journal of Economic Theory* 31: 105–121.

Hagen, E.E. and Hawrylyshyn, O. (1969). "Analysis of world income and growth, 1955–1965." *Economic Development and Cultural Change* 18 (No. 1, Part II): 1–96.

Laitinen, K. (1978). "Why is demand homogeneity so often rejected?" *Economics Letters* 1: 187–191.

Laitinen, K. (1989). *A Theory of the Multiproduct Firm*. Amsterdam and New York: North-Holland Publishing Company.

Laitinen, K. and Theil, H. (1978). "Supply and demand of the multiproduct firm." *European Economic Review* 11: 107–154.

Meisner, J.F. (1979). "The sad fate of the asymptotic Slutsky symmetry test for large systems." *Economics Letters* 2: 231–233.

Raj, B. and Koerts, J. (1992). *Henri Theil's Contributions to Economics and Econometrics*. Three volumes. Dordrecht/Boston/London: Kluwer Academic Publishers.

Shorrocks, A.F. (1980). "The class of additively decomposable inequality measures." *Econometrica* 48: 613–625.

Theil, H. (1950). "A rank-invariant method of linear and polynomical regression analysis." Part I: *Proceedings of the Royal Netherlands Academy of Sciences* 53, pp. 386–392; Part II, ibidem, pp. 521–525; Part III, ibidem, pp. 1397–1412. Also in Raj and Koerts (1992), Ch. 20.

Theil, H. (1951). *De invloed van de voorraden op het consumentengedrag* (Inventories and consumer demand theory). Amsterdam: Poortpers.

Theil, H. (1952). "Qualities, prices, and budget enquiries." *Review of Economic Studies* 19: 129–147. Also in Raj and Koerts (1992), Ch. 34.

Theil, H. (1953a). "Estimation and simultaneous correlation in complete equation systems." Mimeographed memorandum of the Central Planning Bureau, The Hague. Also in Raj and Koerts (1992), Ch. 6.

Theil, H. (1953b). "Enige kwantitatieve aspecten van het probleem der hulpverlening aan onderontwikkelde landen." *De Economist* 101: 721–749.

Theil, H. (1954). *Linear Aggregation of Economic Relations*. Amsterdam: North-Holland Publishing Company.

Theil, H. (1958). *Economic Forecasts and Policy*. Amsterdam: North-Holland Publishing Company. (Second ed. 1961)

Theil, H. (1960). "International inequalities and general criteria for development aid." *International Economic Papers* 10: 42–63. Also in Raj and Koerts (1992), Ch. 48.

Theil, H. (1965). "The information approach to demand analysis." *Econometrica* 33: 67–87. Also in Raj and Koerts (1992), Ch. 36.

Theil, H. (1967). *Economics and Information Theory*. Amsterdam: North-Holland Publishing Company; New York: Elsevier/North-Holland, Inc.

Theil, H. (1975/76). *Theory and Measurement of Consumer Demand*. Two volumes. Amsterdam: North-Holland Publishing Company; New York: Elsevier/North-Holland, Inc.

Theil, H. (1977). "The independent inputs of production." *Econometrica* 45: 1303–1327.

Theil, H. (1979). "World income inequality and its components." *Economics Letters* 2: 99–102. Also in Raj and Koerts (1992), Ch. 52.

Theil, H. (1980a). *The System-Wide Approach to Microeconomics*. Chicago: The University of Chicago Press.

Theil, H. (1980b). *System-Wide Explorations in International Economics, Input-Output Analysis, and Marketing Research*. Amsterdam: North-Holland Publishing Company; New York: Elsevier/North-Holland, Inc.

Theil, H. (1989). "The development of international inequality, 1960–1985." *Journal of Econometrics* 42: 145–155. Also in Raj and Koerts (1992), Ch. 53.

Theil, H. (1990). "Citation classic: Econometric research in the early 1950s." *Current Contents/Social and Behavioral Sciences* 22(17): 24. Also in Raj and Koerts (1992), Vol. I, pp. 26–27.

Theil, H., Chung, C.-F. and Seale, J.L., Jr. (1989). *International Evidence on Consumption Patterns*. Greenwich, Conn.: JAI Press Inc.

Theil, H. and Friedman, Y. (1973). "Regional per capita incomes and income inequalities: Point estimates and their standard errors." *Journal of the American Statistical Association* 68: 531–539.

Theil, H. and Laitinen, K. (1979). "Maximum likelihood estimation of the Rotterdam model under two different conditions." *Economics Letters* 2: 239–244.

Theil, H. and Suhm, F.E. (1981). *International Consumption Comparisons: A System-Wide Approach*. Amsterdam: North-Holland Publishing Company.

Theil, H., Suhm, F.E. and Meisner, J.F. (1980). "Statistical inference in cross-country demand systems." *Economics Letters* 5: 383–387.

United Nations Statistics (1950). *National and Per Capita Incomes of Seventy Countries in 1949, Expressed in U.S. Dollars*. Statistical Papers. Series E, No. 1.

Working, H. (1943). "Statistical laws of family expenditure." *Journal of the American Statistical Association* 38: 43–56.

CHAPTER 2

# The geographic distribution of gross world product, 1950–1990

HENRI THEIL and DONGLING CHEN

**Abstract.** PPP-based data (PPP = purchasing power parity) for gross domestic products are used to assess the affluence of more than 100 non-Communist countries in 1950–1990. A seven-region classification, based on the distinction between temperate and tropical zones, is used to summarize the data on individual countries. The seven regions account for nearly 90 percent of the inequality among these countries in each year. Five journeys around the world are described; the main result is that affluence tends to decline when the traveler moves from temperate zones (in either the Northern or the Southern Hemisphere) toward the Equator. A simple latitude model is developed to explain per capita GDPs; it involves only one parameter, but it accounts for as much as about 70 percent of the variance of the per capita GDPs in each year during the 1970s and 1980s. Another topic considered is that of the G-7 countries, the populations of which are all concentrated in the temperate zones of the Northern Hemisphere.

## 1. The international comparison data

When exchange rates are used to compare the per capita incomes of different countries, two major problems emerge: the results are volatile and they are subject to bias. Volatility arises because exchange rates may be quite variable over time. There is bias in the sense that the poverty of poor nations is overstated. This results from the fact that exchange rates reflect only those goods that are traded internationally. Many goods, particularly services, are not traded internationally or only to a limited extent. Since services tend to be labor intensive, and since labor tends to be relatively cheap in poor countries, the result is that international comparisons based on exchange rates yield a picture that exaggerates the poverty of such countries.

A more satisfactory approach is based on purchasing power parties (PPPs). In fact, the late Irving Kravis and his colleagues at the University of Pennsylvania have been involved in the International Comparison Project (ICP) since the early 1970s to provide PPP-based comparisons. The three paragraphs which follow summarize the procedure of the ICP in a nontechnical manner; for details we refer to Kravis et al. (1975, 1978a, 1982). Our summary is confined to what is needed for a broad understanding of the data used in this article.

The procedure used in the ICP consists of two steps. Each country's gross domestic product (GDP) is divided into more than 100 detailed categories, such as fresh vegetables, and each such category consists of a number of items for which prices are available (such as artichokes and beets in the case of fresh vegetables). The first step of the ICP procedure describes the logarithm of the price of such an item in each country as the sum of an item effect and a country effect, and the antilog of the country effect is an estimated PPP of the detailed category (fresh vegetables in this case).

By dividing the per capita expenditure in national currency on such a detailed category by this PPP we obtain per capita expenditure in real terms. However, such ratios are not additive across categories. To achieve additivity, the ICP uses a second step proposed by Geary (1958) and Khamis (1967, 1970, 1972). This step introduces an overall PPP for each country; "overall" means that this PPP applies to all detailed categories. It also introduces an international price for each detailed category; such a price applies to all countries. This ensures that additivity is obtained. The real GDP data presented in this chapter are all expressed in 1985 international prices.

However, the two steps of the ICP procedure yield data only for one particular year. It is obviously desirable to extend this to a time series consisting of many consecutive years. This was done by Summers and Heston (1984, 1988, 1991, 1993) after an initial attempt by Kravis, Heston and Summers (1978b). To a large extent, the procedure amounts to a statistical reconciliation of cross-country and time-series information. The data used below (known as the Penn World Tables) are from Summers and Heston (1993). Here we use only population and GDP data; we shall sometimes write "income" for GDP when this is more convenient.

We shall not use data for Communist (or formerly Communist) countries, because it has become increasingly clear that such data are highly unreliable.[1] Therefore, it should be understood that our world is the non-Communist world.

## 2. Seven major regions in temperate and tropical zones

The presentation and discussion of four decades of data for dozens of countries are complicated by the sheer size of such a data set. One way of handling this problem is by combining countries into groups of countries, or regions. Indeed, a large proportion of this section is devoted to interesting groupings and their implications. The GDP per capita of a region is obtained simply

[1] China provides an example of how difficult it is to assess GDPs based on purchasing power parties for Communist countries: an article in *The Economist* of 30 April 1994 (p. 78) discusses per capita GDP values for this country in 1990 ranging from 1000 to 2600 dollars. Such a large degree of uncertainty is particularly troublesome for a populous country such as China, since the measures that will be used in this chapter are mostly population-weighted.

by multiplying each country's GDP per capita by its population, summing over all countries of the region, and then dividing the sum by the region's total population.

## 2.1. *Seven regions and their GDPs*

Summers and Heston (1993) provide data for more than 100 countries. Following Theil (1979, 1989) we introduce a number of regions based on a distinction between temperate and tropical zones. There are two regions in the temperate zone: the North and the South. The *North* consists of the USA, Canada, Japan, South Korea and 18 European countries (see the upper part of Table 2-1). The *South* is interpreted as "down under" and consists of six

*Table 2-1.* List of countries

| | | |
|---|---|---|
| | *18 countries in Western Europe* | |
| Austria | Greece | Norway |
| Belgium | Iceland | Portugal |
| Denmark | Ireland | Spain |
| Finland | Italy | Sweden |
| France | Luxembourg | Switzerland |
| Germany (W) | Netherlands | UK |
| | *43 countries in Tropical Africa* | |
| Algeria | Gambia | Nigeria |
| Angola | Ghana | Rwanda |
| Benin | Guinea | Senegal |
| Botswana | Guinea-Bissau | Sierra Leone |
| Burkina Faso | Ivory Coast | Somalia |
| Burundi | Kenya | Swaziland |
| Cameroon | Liberia | Tanzania |
| Cape Verde | Madagascar | Togo |
| Central African Rep. | Malawi | Tunisia |
| Chad | Mali | Uganda |
| Comoros | Mauritania | Zaire |
| Congo | Morocco | Zambia |
| Egypt | Mozambique | Zimbabwe |
| Ethiopia | Namibia | |
| Gabon | Niger | |
| | *22 countries in Tropical America* | |
| Barbados | Guatemala | Paraguay |
| Bolivia | Guyana | Peru |
| Brazil | Haiti | Puerto Rico |
| Colombia | Honduras | Surinam |
| Costa Rica | Jamaica | Trinidad/Tobago |
| Dominican Rep. | Mexico | Venezuela |
| Ecuador | Nicaragua | |
| El Salvador | Panama | |

countries: Australia, New Zealand, Chile, Argentina, Uruguay, South Africa. The dividing line that we choose between temperate and tropical zones is the 30th parallels North and South (the so-called *horse latitudes*) except that we use the Mediterranean Sea (which is more North than the 30th parallel) as the separation between Europe and Africa. Most of Australia is North of its 30th parallel, but we feel justified in allocating this country to the temperate zone because the vast majority of Australians live South of that parallel.

One region in the tropical zone is *Tropical Africa*. It consists of 43 countries North of S. Africa and South of the Mediterranean Sea (see the middle part of Table 2-1). Another is *Tropical America*, which consists of 22 countries South of the USA, including the Caribbean area, all the way down to Brazil and Paraguay (see the lower part of Table 2-1).

Theil (1979, 1989) used Tropical Asia as the third tropical region, but here we divide into this three so that there are seven regions as a whole. *South-East Asia* consists of eight countries: Hong Kong, Indonesia, Malaysia, Papua New Guinea, Philippines, Singapore, Taiwan, Thailand. *South-Central Asia* consists of six countries: Bangladesh, India, Myanmar (Burma), Nepal, Pakistan, Sri Lanka. *South-West Asia* also consists of six countries: Iran, Iraq, Israel, Jordan, Syria, Turkey. As a whole, the seven regions contain 113 countries. The Summers-Heston data cover several more, particularly small island nations, but we shall find it convenient to ignore these in this section.

The per capita GDPs of the seven regions, together with that of the USA (shown here for comparison purposes), are given in Table 2-2 for the period 1950–1990, although missing data for a number of countries imply shorter periods for most regions. Figure 2-1 presents a picture, based on the numbers of Table 2-2, on a logarithmic scale. It is obvious that there are substantial differences among regions. In particular, Figure 2-1 clearly shows that there is a well-defined hierarchy among the seven regions except for two (approximate) ties:

1, North (which includes the USA).
2, South ("down under").
3/4, (tie), Tropical America and South-West Asia. The figures for South-West Asia would have been somewhat higher if the oil countries in the Arabian Peninsula had been represented more extensively.
5, South-East Asia. Note that this region's per capita GDP has been subject to a sizeable upward trend.
6/7, (tie), Tropical Africa and South-Central Asia.

## 2.2. *An inequality analysis*

Our next topic is an inequality analysis for countries and regions. For this purpose we confine ourselves to the period 1961–1986 during which data for all 113 countries are available. Our measure of inequality is the natural logarithm of the ratio of arithmetic mean income to geometric mean income.

*Table 2-2.* GDP per capita: USA and seven regions[a]

| Year (1) | USA (2) | North (3) | South (4) | Trop. Africa (5) | Trop. America (6) | South Asia West (7) | South Asia Central (8) | South Asia East (9) |
|---|---|---|---|---|---|---|---|---|
| 1950 | 8625 | . | 3413 | . | . | . | . | . |
| 51 | 8987 | . | 3450 | . | . | . | . | . |
| 52 | 8998 | . | 3245 | . | . | . | . | . |
| 53 | 9226 | 5181 | 3416 | . | . | . | . | . |
| 54 | 9006 | 5236 | 3575 | . | . | . | . | . |
| 55 | 9593 | 5572 | 3675 | . | . | . | . | . |
| 56 | 9584 | 5698 | 3634 | . | . | . | . | . |
| 57 | 9530 | 5780 | 3724 | . | . | . | . | . |
| 58 | 9278 | 5754 | 3824 | . | . | . | . | . |
| 59 | 9718 | 6020 | 3774 | . | . | . | . | . |
| 1960 | 9776 | 6249 | 3863 | . | 2123 | 2129 | 669 | 878 |
| 61 | 9835 | 6466 | 3926 | 693 | 2185 | 2143 | 648 | 907 |
| 62 | 10234 | 6729 | 3974 | 703 | 2254 | 2229 | 658 | 927 |
| 63 | 10514 | 6981 | 4041 | 732 | 2286 | 2258 | 700 | 931 |
| 64 | 10928 | 7341 | 4271 | 751 | 2389 | 2404 | 727 | 958 |
| 65 | 11492 | 7648 | 4382 | 761 | 2415 | 2537 | 692 | 980 |
| 66 | 11999 | 7977 | 4482 | 758 | 2478 | 2646 | 643 | 1013 |
| 67 | 12160 | 8200 | 4539 | 749 | 2543 | 2677 | 674 | 1045 |
| 68 | 12555 | 8592 | 4715 | 772 | 2671 | 2901 | 692 | 1090 |
| 69 | 12806 | 8967 | 4921 | 817 | 2757 | 3037 | 715 | 1149 |
| 1970 | 12725 | 9197 | 5121 | 864 | 2903 | 3199 | 746 | 1218 |
| 71 | 13041 | 9464 | 5272 | 897 | 3019 | 3311 | 728 | 1256 |
| 72 | 13632 | 9903 | 5299 | 908 | 3170 | 3515 | 703 | 1310 |
| 73 | 14226 | 10408 | 5428 | 922 | 3367 | 3696 | 721 | 1421 |
| 74 | 13909 | 10339 | 5536 | 955 | 3538 | 3871 | 713 | 1481 |
| 75 | 13479 | 10122 | 5400 | 972 | 3597 | 4029 | 753 | 1522 |
| 76 | 14087 | 10570 | 5381 | 993 | 3758 | 4418 | 753 | 1601 |
| 77 | 14655 | 10896 | 5371 | 1044 | 3818 | 4574 | 796 | 1696 |
| 78 | 15303 | 11285 | 5435 | 1068 | 3917 | 4137 | 826 | 1819 |
| 79 | 15408 | 11577 | 5595 | 1053 | 4077 | 4158 | 792 | 1933 |
| 1980 | 15097 | 11582 | 5755 | 1067 | 4250 | 3693 | 830 | 2033 |
| 81 | 15339 | 11677 | 5788 | 1085 | 4208 | 3493 | 845 | 2179 |
| 82 | 14612 | 11499 | 5393 | 1064 | 4041 | 3535 | 858 | 2199 |
| 83 | 15039 | 11749 | 5417 | 1028 | 3777 | 3763 | 897 | 2298 |
| 84 | 16154 | 12302 | 5591 | 1009 | 3821 | 3753 | 917 | 2336 |
| 85 | 16559 | 12655 | 5483 | 1008 | 3908 | 3735 | 956 | 2324 |
| 86 | 16885 | 12972 | 5558 | 1015 | 3961 | 3595 | 982 | 2374 |
| 87 | 17332 | 13376 | 5670 | . | 3976 | 3537 | . | 2497 |
| 88 | 17975 | 13962 | 5712 | . | . | . | . | 2643 |
| 89 | 18354 | 14388 | 5691 | . | . | . | . | 2809 |
| 1990 | 18309 | . | 5502 | . | . | . | . | 2987 |

[a] Expressed in 1985 international prices. Dots indicate missing observations for one or more countries in the region.

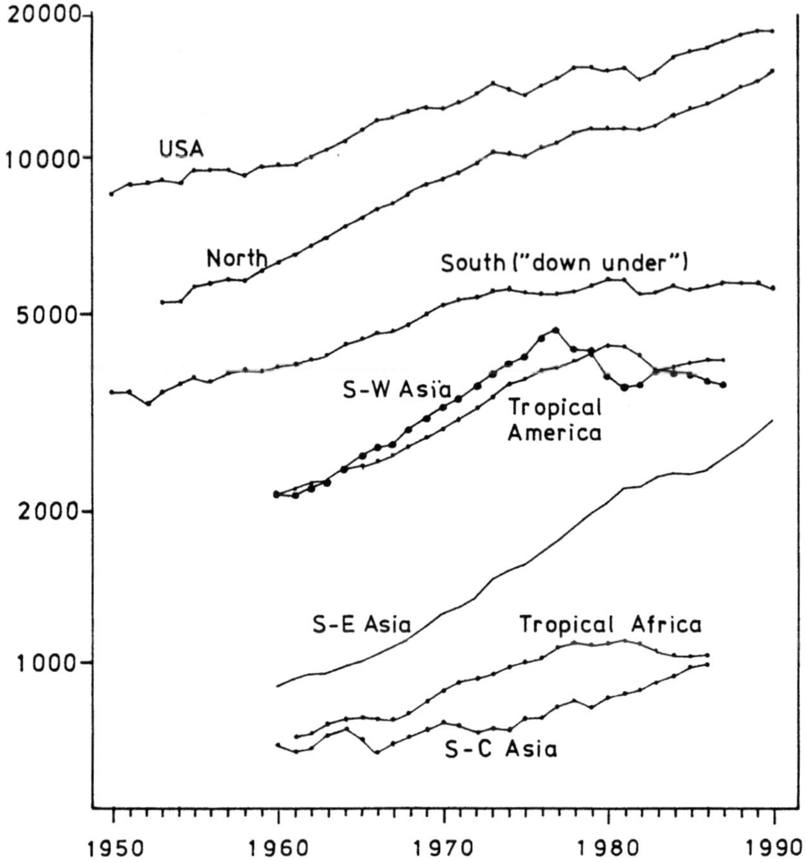


*Figure 2-1.* GDP per capita, 1950–1990: USA and seven regions.

When this measure is applied to the 113 countries, it can be written as

$$J = \sum_{i=1}^{113} p_i \log_e (p_i/y_i)$$

where $p_i$ is the population share and $y_i$ the income share of country $i$. (Here and elsewhere, income is identified with GDP.) Regional inequality is then defined as

$$J_R = \sum_{g=1}^{7} P_g \log_e (P_g/Y_g)$$

where $P_g = \Sigma_i p_i$ and $Y_g = \Sigma_i y_i$ (sums over $i \in R_g$) are the population and income shares of region $R_g$. The regional population shares are shown in Table 2-3 at five-year intervals. Note that the population shares of the two richest regions decline (columns 3 and 4), while those of the five poorest regions all increase (columns 5 to 9).

*Table 2-3.* Population by regions

| | | Percentage shares | | | | | | |
|---|---|---|---|---|---|---|---|---|
| | | | | | | South Asia | | |
| Year (1) | World (millions) (2) | North (3) | South (4) | Trop. Africa (5) | Trop. America (6) | West (7) | Central (8) | East (9) |
| 1961 | 1973 | 32.1 | 3.18 | 13.3 | 9.4 | 3.29 | 29.7 | 9.07 |
| 1966 | 2190 | 30.6 | 3.15 | 13.6 | 9.8 | 3.43 | 30.1 | 9.30 |
| 1971 | 2423 | 29.0 | 3.12 | 13.9 | 10.1 | 3.60 | 30.7 | 9.52 |
| 1976 | 2679 | 27.4 | 3.09 | 14.3 | 10.4 | 3.75 | 31.2 | 9.75 |
| 1981 | 2954 | 25.8 | 3.04 | 14.9 | 10.7 | 3.91 | 31.8 | 9.87 |
| 1986 | 3253 | 24.1 | 3.00 | 15.7 | 10.8 | 4.13 | 32.3 | 9.90 |

Similarly, the inequality among the countries of region $R_g$ is

$$J_g = \sum_{i \in R_g} (p_i/P_g) \log_e [(p_i/P_g)/(y_i/Y_g)]$$

and the relationship between the $J$'s is $J = J_R + \bar{J}$ with $\bar{J}$ defined as the average within-region inequality:

$$\bar{J} = \sum_{g=1}^{7} P_g J_g$$

Table 2-4 shows $J$ (international inequality), $J_R$ and $\bar{J}$ in columns 2 to 4. International inequality increases from about 0.57 in the early 1960s to about 0.65 in the later 1960s, after which it remains approximately constant. Most of the inequality among countries is regional in nature. This matter is pursued in column 5, which expresses $J_R$ as a percentage of $J$. This percentage increases slowly from about 87 in the early 1960s to almost 90 in the mid-1970s, after which it declines to about 88 in the mid-1980s. Note that these percentages are all much higher than those given in Theil (1989) for five regions; the latter fluctuate between 73 and 80. The main reason is, of course, the division of the heterogeneous Tropical Asia region into three more homogeneous regions. (There is also a minor difference caused by the different country coverages of the two studies.)

The average within-region inequality $\bar{J}$ is shown in column 4 of the Table 2-4. It fluctuates within rather narrow bounds, between 0.065 and 0.08, and its 1986 value is almost equal to that of 1961. However, in spite of this near-constancy it is not true that the contributions of the regions to $\bar{J}$ have been stable. It follows from the definition of $\bar{J}$ that $P_g J_g/\bar{J}$ may be viewed as the proportion of $\bar{J}$ that is attributable to region $R_g$. These components in percentage form are shown in Table 2-5. In the early 1960s, the North accounted for more than 50 percent of $\bar{J}$, Tropical Africa for almost 20 percent, and all other regions for less than 10 percent each. But this picture changes quickly.

*Table 2-4.* International and regional inequality

| Year (1) | International inequality (2) | Regional inequality (3) | Average within-region inequality (4) | (3) as a percentage of (2) (5) |
|---|---|---|---|---|
| 1961 | 0.5665 | 0.4902 | 0.0762 | 86.5 |
| 1962 | 0.5740 | 0.4992 | 0.0749 | 87.0 |
| 1963 | 0.5714 | 0.4954 | 0.0760 | 86.7 |
| 1964 | 0.5787 | 0.5023 | 0.0765 | 86.8 |
| 1965 | 0.6081 | 0.5275 | 0.0806 | 86.7 |
| 1966 | 0.6403 | 0.5606 | 0.0798 | 87.6 |
| 1967 | 0.6398 | 0.5597 | 0.0801 | 87.5 |
| 1968 | 0.6451 | 0.5662 | 0.0789 | 87.8 |
| 1969 | 0.6414 | 0.5667 | 0.0747 | 88.4 |
| 1970 | 0.6271 | 0.5562 | 0.0709 | 88.7 |
| 1971 | 0.6346 | 0.5677 | 0.0668 | 89.5 |
| 1972 | 0.6591 | 0.5909 | 0.0682 | 89.7 |
| 1973 | 0.6665 | 0.5980 | 0.0684 | 89.7 |
| 1974 | 0.6568 | 0.5905 | 0.0663 | 89.9 |
| 1975 | 0.6287 | 0.5636 | 0.0651 | 89.6 |
| 1976 | 0.6448 | 0.5758 | 0.0687 | 89.3 |
| 1977 | 0.6349 | 0.5653 | 0.0696 | 89.0 |
| 1978 | 0.6343 | 0.5637 | 0.0706 | 88.9 |
| 1979 | 0.6562 | 0.5832 | 0.0730 | 88.9 |
| 1980 | 0.6408 | 0.5672 | 0.0736 | 88.5 |
| 1981 | 0.6313 | 0.5609 | 0.0704 | 88.8 |
| 1982 | 0.6205 | 0.5512 | 0.0692 | 88.8 |
| 1983 | 0.6217 | 0.5508 | 0.0708 | 88.6 |
| 1984 | 0.6411 | 0.5660 | 0.0751 | 88.3 |
| 1985 | 0.6444 | 0.5670 | 0.0773 | 88.0 |
| 1986 | 0.6447 | 0.5691 | 0.0756 | 88.3 |

The contribution of the North declined sharply, from more than 50 percent in 1961 and 1962 to only 15 percent in 1986, partly because of its declining population share $P_g$ (see column 3 of Table 2-3) but more importantly because of its declining inequality $J_g$ caused by the fact that the rest of the North caught up with the USA. At the same time there was an increase in the inequality $J_g$ among the nations of Tropical Africa and South-East Asia. The result is that in the mid-1980s Tropical Africa accounted for more than 40 percent of $\bar{J}$ and South-East Asia for almost 20 percent, leaving the North in third position.

## 2.3. *Subregions: Western Europe further considered*

The extension of the regional analysis to subregions is straightforward, which may be illustrated briefly for the 18 countries of Western Europe. Recall that these countries are part of the North, along with the USA, Canada, Japan

*Table 2-5.* Components of the average within-region inequality[a]

| Year (1) | North (2) | South (3) | Trop. Africa (4) | Trop. America (5) | South Asia West (6) | South Asia Central (7) | South Asia East (8) |
|---|---|---|---|---|---|---|---|
| 1961 | 51.5 | 4.7 | 19.2 | 9.5 | 2.0 | 6.2 | 7.0 |
| 1962 | 51.6 | 5.0 | 17.4 | 9.8 | 2.0 | 5.5 | 8.7 |
| 1963 | 47.3 | 5.1 | 19.1 | 10.6 | 1.7 | 5.0 | 11.2 |
| 1964 | 45.2 | 5.1 | 19.7 | 11.6 | 1.9 | 5.0 | 11.5 |
| 1965 | 43.4 | 4.6 | 18.0 | 11.8 | 2.4 | 7.0 | 12.9 |
| 1966 | 41.7 | 4.7 | 17.4 | 11.5 | 2.1 | 8.6 | 14.0 |
| 1967 | 38.5 | 4.5 | 19.5 | 11.7 | 1.8 | 9.2 | 14.7 |
| 1968 | 35.8 | 5.0 | 21.9 | 11.4 | 2.4 | 8.6 | 14.9 |
| 1969 | 34.7 | 5.1 | 21.2 | 12.0 | 2.5 | 8.8 | 15.8 |
| 1970 | 31.8 | 5.1 | 22.8 | 12.2 | 3.3 | 7.4 | 17.4 |
| 1971 | 32.0 | 5.3 | 22.6 | 11.7 | 3.1 | 6.1 | 19.2 |
| 1972 | 31.1 | 5.5 | 24.6 | 10.8 | 3.1 | 5.1 | 19.8 |
| 1973 | 28.7 | 5.7 | 24.9 | 10.0 | 4.0 | 6.6 | 20.1 |
| 1974 | 27.1 | 5.5 | 26.5 | 10.1 | 3.5 | 8.0 | 19.3 |
| 1975 | 25.8 | 6.1 | 28.8 | 10.7 | 3.1 | 7.6 | 17.9 |
| 1976 | 23.7 | 6.1 | 30.6 | 10.0 | 3.1 | 7.8 | 18.6 |
| 1977 | 22.9 | 5.7 | 32.1 | 9.8 | 3.0 | 7.3 | 19.1 |
| 1978 | 22.0 | 5.9 | 32.7 | 10.1 | 2.2 | 8.2 | 18.9 |
| 1979 | 19.7 | 5.4 | 33.0 | 10.4 | 3.5 | 9.4 | 18.6 |
| 1980 | 19.3 | 5.1 | 34.5 | 10.1 | 3.1 | 9.3 | 18.7 |
| 1981 | 20.2 | 5.3 | 36.7 | 11.5 | 1.6 | 7.6 | 17.0 |
| 1982 | 17.6 | 5.8 | 38.6 | 11.0 | 1.4 | 7.8 | 17.7 |
| 1983 | 16.8 | 6.6 | 40.2 | 10.2 | 1.7 | 7.2 | 17.3 |
| 1984 | 16.8 | 6.2 | 41.2 | 9.8 | 1.4 | 6.6 | 18.1 |
| 1985 | 15.9 | 6.8 | 42.0 | 10.0 | 1.2 | 7.0 | 17.3 |
| 1986 | 15.1 | 6.8 | 41.4 | 9.8 | 0.9 | 7.4 | 18.6 |

[a] Components expressed as percentages.

and South Korea. Here we divide these 18 countries into three groups, based on their position with respect to the European Union. One region is *non-EU*, consisting of six countries: Austria, Finland, Iceland, Norway, Sweden, Switzerland. Another is the *EU Center*, consisting of eight countries: Belgium, Denmark, France, Germany (W), Italy, Luxembourg, Netherlands, UK. The third is the *EU Periphery*, consisting of four countries: Greece, Ireland, Portugal, Spain.

Columns 2 to 5 of Table 2-6 show the per capita GDPs of Western Europe and its three regions. Figure 2-2 illustrates these results graphically, using the same scale as that of Figure 2-1. Western Europe's per capita GDP was always below that of the USA, but it increased faster. Similarly, the per capita GDP of non-EU exceeded that of EU Center and the latter exceeded that of EU Periphery in every year, but the Periphery's increase was faster, at least until the mid-1970s, suggesting a convergence of affluence.

*Table 2-6.* GDP per capita and international inequality in Western Europe

| | GDP per capita[a] | | | | Inequality | | |
|---|---|---|---|---|---|---|---|
| Year (1) | All 18 countries (2) | non-EU (3) | EU Center (4) | EU Periphery (5) | All 18 countries (6) | Regional (7) | Av. within region (8) |
| 1950 | 3707 | 4721 | 4009 | 1775 | 0.0683 | 0.0406 | 0.0277 |
| 51 | 3902 | 4931 | 4196 | 1994 | 0.0598 | 0.0346 | 0.0251 |
| 52 | 3999 | 4990 | 4307 | 2053 | 0.0563 | 0.0341 | 0.0222 |
| 53 | 4158 | 5083 | 4514 | 2031 | 0.0578 | 0.0383 | 0.0196 |
| 54 | 4363 | 5402 | 4707 | 2225 | 0.0548 | 0.0346 | 0.0202 |
| 55 | 4621 | 5700 | 4995 | 2326 | 0.0544 | 0.0357 | 0.0188 |
| 56 | 4799 | 5889 | 5181 | 2462 | 0.0522 | 0.0339 | 0.0183 |
| 57 | 4942 | 6036 | 5335 | 2549 | 0.0505 | 0.0334 | 0.0171 |
| 58 | 4999 | 6020 | 5396 | 2629 | 0.0472 | 0.0315 | 0.0157 |
| 59 | 5207 | 6324 | 5643 | 2595 | 0.0506 | 0.0362 | 0.0144 |
| 1960 | 5532 | 6738 | 5991 | 2778 | 0.0493 | 0.0357 | 0.0136 |
| 61 | 5805 | 7124 | 6244 | 3077 | 0.0437 | 0.0311 | 0.0127 |
| 62 | 6017 | 7322 | 6453 | 3306 | 0.0408 | 0.0280 | 0.0128 |
| 63 | 6239 | 7585 | 6663 | 3556 | 0.0369 | 0.0251 | 0.0118 |
| 64 | 6559 | 7976 | 7004 | 3738 | 0.0380 | 0.0251 | 0.0130 |
| 65 | 6783 | 8222 | 7219 | 3987 | 0.0358 | 0.0227 | 0.0131 |
| 66 | 6985 | 8402 | 7421 | 4202 | 0.0333 | 0.0210 | 0.0124 |
| 67 | 7181 | 8608 | 7622 | 4373 | 0.0306 | 0.0201 | 0.0105 |
| 68 | 7508 | 8825 | 7976 | 4644 | 0.0285 | 0.0189 | 0.0097 |
| 69 | 7919 | 9271 | 8395 | 5005 | 0.0277 | 0.0174 | 0.0103 |
| 1970 | 8216 | 9727 | 8688 | 5222 | 0.0275 | 0.0171 | 0.0104 |
| 71 | 8472 | 9954 | 8950 | 5450 | 0.0248 | 0.0161 | 0.0087 |
| 72 | 8828 | 10296 | 9296 | 5861 | 0.0226 | 0.0141 | 0.0085 |
| 73 | 9282 | 10690 | 9758 | 6318 | 0.0196 | 0.0126 | 0.0071 |
| 74 | 9388 | 11010 | 9819 | 6529 | 0.0185 | 0.0116 | 0.0069 |
| 75 | 9167 | 10846 | 9565 | 6465 | 0.0183 | 0.0111 | 0.0072 |
| 76 | 9568 | 10977 | 10065 | 6611 | 0.0188 | 0.0120 | 0.0068 |
| 77 | 9755 | 11091 | 10286 | 6720 | 0.0185 | 0.0122 | 0.0062 |
| 78 | 9988 | 11181 | 10586 | 6764 | 0.0190 | 0.0133 | 0.0057 |
| 79 | 10336 | 11694 | 11002 | 6759 | 0.0205 | 0.0157 | 0.0049 |
| 1980 | 10462 | 12148 | 11112 | 6802 | 0.0208 | 0.0163 | 0.0045 |
| 81 | 10357 | 12107 | 11003 | 6707 | 0.0210 | 0.0168 | 0.0042 |
| 82 | 10400 | 12144 | 11049 | 6756 | 0.0204 | 0.0166 | 0.0038 |
| 83 | 10530 | 12369 | 11205 | 6743 | 0.0214 | 0.0177 | 0.0037 |
| 84 | 10751 | 12738 | 11463 | 6755 | 0.0231 | 0.0192 | 0.0039 |
| 85 | 10987 | 13117 | 11706 | 6898 | 0.0231 | 0.0194 | 0.0037 |
| 86 | 11291 | 13414 | 12034 | 7106 | 0.0229 | 0.0192 | 0.0037 |
| 87 | 11612 | 13712 | 12342 | 7487 | 0.0210 | 0.0174 | 0.0036 |
| 88 | 12083 | 14072 | 12841 | 7902 | 0.0199 | 0.0163 | 0.0036 |
| 89 | 12475 | 14470 | 13221 | 8328 | 0.0186 | 0.0149 | 0.0037 |
| 1990 | 12755 | 14623 | 13506 | 8637 | 0.0179 | 0.0138 | 0.0041 |

[a]Expressed in 1985 international prices.

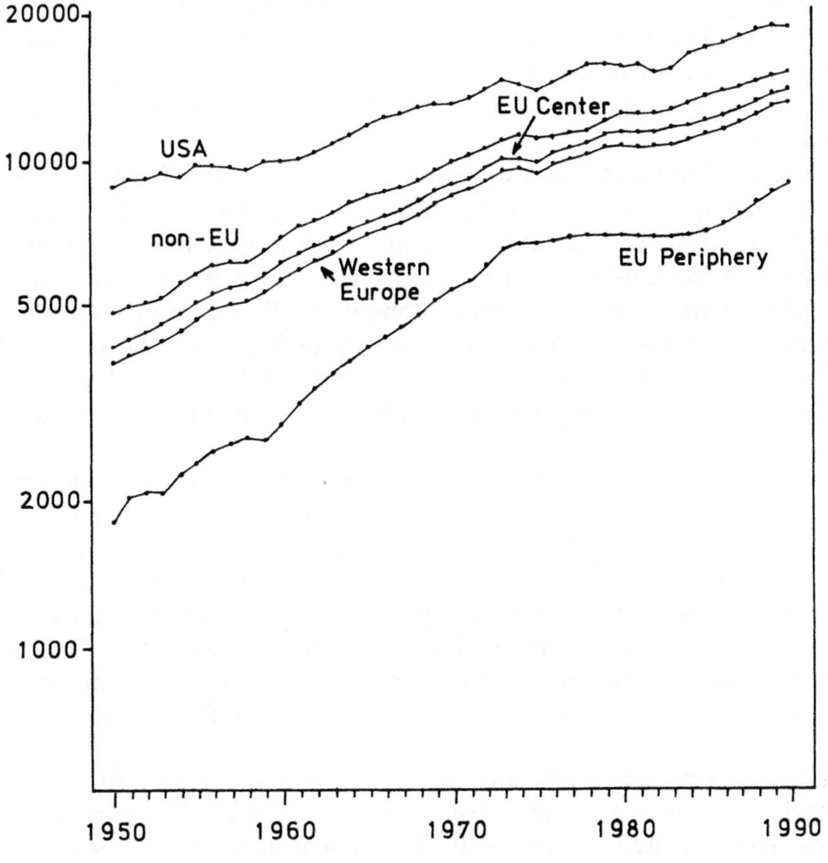


*Figure 2-2.* GDP per capita, 1950–1990: USA and Western Europe.

The last three columns of Table 2-6 pursue the matter of convergence more systematically. We use the same measure of inequality ($J$, $J_R$, $J_g$, $\bar{J}$) as in Section 2.2, but now for 18 countries rather than 113 and three regions rather than seven. The international inequality (column 6) shows a substantial decline, from almost 0.07 in 1950 to less than 0.02 in 1990. The regional component (column 7) dominates the average within-region component (column 8) in each year. The latter component declined from 1950 to 1980, after which it stabilized. For more details see Theil and Seale (1994).

## 2.4. *Kuznets' hypothesis of divergence-convergence*

Kuznets (1955) hypothesized that, as an agrarian society becomes more urbanized and affluent, income inequality initially increases and then decreases (divergence followed by convergence). Can the data discussed here confirm or deny such a hypothesis? It is true that Kuznets discusses inequality within one country, not across countries, but several authors have extended the divergence-convergence hypothesis to the cross-country level. For example, Paukert (1973), Ahluwalia (1976), Papanek and Kyn (1986) and Ram (1989) have used cross-country data to test Kuznets' divergence-convergence hypothesis.

Table 2-6 (columns 2 and 6) shows that in the period 1950–1990, when Western Europe's per capita GDP increased from less than 4000 to almost 13000, its inequality declined substantially. During that same period both non-EU and EU Center saw their per capita GDPs rise from between 4000 and 5000 to about 14000 (columns 3 and 4), while the inequalities of both regions (not shown here) declined by more than 90 percent. Since these two regions may be viewed as affluent, the decrease of their inequalities may be regarded as evidence in favor of the convergence component of Kuznets' hypothesis.

Also, column 5 of Table 2-6 shows that during the 20-year period 1950–1970 the EU Periphery's per capita GDP increased from less than 2000 to about 5000. During that period the inequality of this region (not shown here) fluctuated without any clear trend; the downward trend of this inequality emerged only after 1970 when the region's per capita GDP increased further until about 8600 (see column 5). It is not difficult to argue that the first 20 years provide evidence of the transition from the divergence component to the convergence component of Kuznets' hypothesis. See Theil and Seale (1994) for further details.

These two authors considered several other regions as well. The most intriguing case is that of sub-Saharan Africa. In the 1970s that region's per capita GDP increased, but the 1980s showed a decreasing trend; sub-Saharan Africa's per capita GDP in the late 1980s was less than in 1970. The region's inequality tends to increase from the mid-1960s until the late 1970s, and to decline thereafter. But we may argue that this is precisely what Kuznets' hypothesis would lead us to expect, since the former period (until the late 1970s) is characterized by positive growth and the latter by negative growth. Of course, the irony is that negative growth was not included in Kuznets' original formulation.

## 3. Five journeys around the world

In the previous section we combined countries into regions. In the present section we shall consider both regions and individual countries.

### 3.1. *A different view of Western Europe*

Recall that we have 18 countries in Western Europe. We define *Europe's core* as the seven-country region consisting of UK, France, Switzerland, Germany (W) and the three Benelux countries. This core is the area through which Western Europe's major rivers (Rhine, Meuse, Thames, Seine, Rhone) are flowing, with their tributaries and connecting canals. The other 11 countries are located either North or South or West or East of the core as shown below.

| | *West* | *Central* | *East* |
|---|---|---|---|
| *North* | Iceland | Denmark, Norway, Sweden | Finland |
| *Central* | Ireland | Europe's core (see text) | Austria |
| *South* | Portugal, Spain | Italy | Greece |

Column 2 of Table 2-7 gives the per capita GDP of Europe's core. The next 11 columns contain the per capita GDPs of the 11 European countries outside the core, starting in the North-West (Iceland) and then moving clockwise. The figures in these columns express the per capita GDP as a percentage of the core's per capita GDP in the same year. We shall refer to these figures as *GDP ratios*; such ratios enable us to trace the country's economic development relative to that of Europe's core.

Column 2 shows that the core's per capita GDP increased almost uninterruptedly, from 4400 in 1950 to nearly 13900 in 1990, or more than threefold. Columns 3 to 7 indicate that living in the North was no obstacle to a good life, particularly in the North-Central, although the Danes and Swedes lost some ground relative to Europe's core after starting at a high level. Austria (column 8) had a GDP ratio of about two-thirds in the early 1950s, but it managed to improve this to about 90 percent in the mid-1970s and slightly higher in later years.

Greece, Spain and Portugal (columns 9, 11, 12) have GDP ratios that are definitely on the low side in the early 1950s. A comparison with columns 3 to 7 shows that the standard of living in Southern Europe is much lower than in Northern Europe. Italy (column 10) seems an exception, but we should recognize that much of Italy is not very Southern; Northern Italy (down to Florence) is at the same latitude as Southern France.[2] Note that the GDP ratios of all four Southern European countries (columns 9 to 12) are much higher in 1990 than in 1950.

Ireland (column 13) presents a different picture. Its GDP ratio was 60 percent in 1950 (almost equal to that of Austria and Italy), after which it *declined* to about 50 percent in the mid-1950s, where it remained during more than a decade. It went up in the early 1970s and it was 65 percent in 1990.

[2] Using regional data within countries, we can add Northern Italy to Europe's core (and also Catalonia, and perhaps delete Northern Ireland and Scotland). However, such exercises are beyond the scope of this chapter.

*Table 2-7.* GDP per capita: Europe's core and surrounding countries[a]

| Year (1) | Core (2) | Iceland (3) | Denmark (4) | Norway (5) | Sweden (6) | Finland (7) | Austria (8) | Greece (9) |
|---|---|---|---|---|---|---|---|---|
| 1950 | 4400 | 90 | 120 | 100 | 131 | 81 | 67 | 32 |
| 51 | 4603 | 83 | 110 | 96 | 126 | 85 | 69 | 32 |
| 52 | 4707 | 78 | 108 | 98 | 127 | 86 | 67 | 31 |
| 53 | 4910 | 85 | 110 | 99 | 123 | 80 | 66 | 32 |
| 54 | 5135 | 87 | 108 | 98 | 124 | 84 | 69 | 32 |
| 55 | 5458 | 90 | 100 | 94 | 120 | 84 | 72 | 31 |
| 56 | 5669 | 86 | 98 | 92 | 118 | 82 | 72 | 32 |
| 57 | 5829 | 82 | 99 | 92 | 117 | 80 | 74 | 33 |
| 58 | 5853 | 87 | 100 | 92 | 119 | 79 | 76 | 34 |
| 59 | 6107 | 85 | 104 | 90 | 119 | 80 | 75 | 34 |
| 1960 | 6458 | 80 | 105 | 88 | 116 | 83 | 80 | 32 |
| 61 | 6691 | 76 | 107 | 88 | 117 | 86 | 81 | 35 |
| 62 | 6873 | 78 | 109 | 89 | 118 | 85 | 80 | 34 |
| 63 | 7070 | 83 | 105 | 91 | 120 | 84 | 81 | 36 |
| 64 | 7476 | 83 | 109 | 90 | 121 | 83 | 80 | 37 |
| 65 | 7717 | 84 | 109 | 91 | 120 | 86 | 80 | 40 |
| 66 | 7887 | 89 | 109 | 93 | 119 | 85 | 82 | 40 |
| 67 | 8030 | 86 | 109 | 95 | 120 | 84 | 83 | 41 |
| 68 | 8383 | 77 | 108 | 92 | 118 | 82 | 82 | 42 |
| 69 | 8805 | 73 | 109 | 91 | 117 | 85 | 82 | 44 |
| 1970 | 9089 | 78 | 106 | 89 | 117 | 91 | 83 | 47 |
| 71 | 9422 | 86 | 105 | 90 | 113 | 89 | 84 | 48 |
| 72 | 9823 | 84 | 105 | 90 | 110 | 90 | 85 | 50 |
| 73 | 10257 | 85 | 104 | 89 | 109 | 92 | 85 | 51 |
| 74 | 10236 | 90 | 102 | 94 | 113 | 96 | 88 | 49 |
| 75 | 10000 | 92 | 102 | 99 | 118 | 98 | 90 | 52 |
| 76 | 10459 | 90 | 104 | 101 | 114 | 91 | 90 | 52 |
| 77 | 10694 | 96 | 103 | 102 | 108 | 89 | 92 | 52 |
| 78 | 11001 | 98 | 101 | 103 | 106 | 87 | 89 | 53 |
| 79 | 11379 | 99 | 100 | 104 | 106 | 91 | 90 | 52 |
| 1980 | 11406 | 104 | 98 | 107 | 108 | 96 | 93 | 52 |
| 81 | 11291 | 108 | 97 | 109 | 108 | 98 | 93 | 52 |
| 82 | 11343 | 108 | 100 | 108 | 108 | 100 | 93 | 52 |
| 83 | 11531 | 99 | 101 | 111 | 108 | 100 | 93 | 51 |
| 84 | 11772 | 101 | 105 | 115 | 110 | 101 | 93 | 51 |
| 85 | 12014 | 101 | 107 | 118 | 111 | 101 | 93 | 51 |
| 86 | 12348 | 104 | 109 | 120 | 110 | 99 | 92 | 50 |
| 87 | 12653 | 108 | 106 | 118 | 110 | 101 | 91 | 49 |
| 88 | 13168 | 102 | 102 | 112 | 108 | 103 | 91 | 49 |
| 89 | 13565 | 97 | 100 | 108 | 107 | 106 | 91 | 49 |
| 1990 | 13874 | 93 | 99 | 107 | 104 | 102 | 93 | 48 |

[a] The entries in column 2 are in 1985 international prices; those in all other columns express the per capita GDP as a percentage of the core value (column 2) in the same year.

| Italy (10) | Spain (11) | Portugal (12) | Ireland (13) | Turkey (14) | S-W Asia[b] (15) | North Africa (16) | N-s-S Africa[c] (17) | Year (18) |
|---|---|---|---|---|---|---|---|---|
| 64 | 44 | 27 | 60 | 24 | . | . | . | 1950 |
| 65 | 49 | 29 | 59 | 27 | . | . | . | 51 |
| 66 | 50 | 29 | 58 | 28 | . | . | . | 52 |
| 68 | 46 | 30 | 57 | 30 | . | . | . | 53 |
| 67 | 50 | 29 | 55 | 26 | . | . | . | 54 |
| 67 | 49 | 28 | 54 | 26 | . | . | . | 55 |
| 67 | 50 | 28 | 51 | 25 | . | . | . | 56 |
| 67 | 50 | 29 | 49 | 28 | . | . | . | 57 |
| 69 | 52 | 29 | 49 | 30 | . | . | . | 58 |
| 70 | 48 | 29 | 50 | 27 | . | . | . | 59 |
| 72 | 49 | 29 | 49 | 25 | 39 | 15 | . | 1960 |
| 75 | 53 | 30 | 50 | 24 | 38 | 15 | . | 61 |
| 77 | 57 | 30 | 51 | 24 | 39 | 14 | . | 62 |
| 79 | 60 | 31 | 51 | 25 | 37 | 15 | . | 63 |
| 76 | 59 | 30 | 51 | 24 | 38 | 16 | . | 64 |
| 75 | 61 | 31 | 50 | 23 | 40 | 15 | . | 65 |
| 77 | 63 | 31 | 49 | 25 | 40 | 14 | . | 66 |
| 81 | 64 | 33 | 50 | 25 | 40 | 14 | . | 67 |
| 82 | 65 | 35 | 52 | 25 | 42 | 15 | . | 68 |
| 83 | 67 | 34 | 53 | 24 | 42 | 15 | . | 69 |
| 84 | 66 | 37 | 54 | 24 | 43 | 15 | . | 1970 |
| 82 | 66 | 40 | 51 | 25 | 42 | 14 | 9.2 | 71 |
| 80 | 68 | 41 | 51 | 25 | 44 | 14 | 8.4 | 72 |
| 82 | 69 | 44 | 55 | 24 | 45 | 14 | 7.1 | 73 |
| 86 | 73 | 46 | 56 | 26 | 46 | 14 | 7.3 | 74 |
| 84 | 74 | 44 | 58 | 28 | 49 | 16 | 7.9 | 75 |
| 85 | 72 | 43 | 56 | 29 | 52 | 16 | 8.1 | 76 |
| 85 | 71 | 44 | 58 | 29 | 52 | 16 | 8.8 | 77 |
| 85 | 69 | 43 | 60 | 27 | 44 | 16 | 8.4 | 78 |
| 87 | 66 | 43 | 60 | 26 | 44 | 17 | 7.6 | 79 |
| 92 | 66 | 44 | 59 | 25 | 37 | 17 | 7.5 | 1980 |
| 92 | 65 | 45 | 62 | 25 | 35 | 18 | 7.5 | 81 |
| 91 | 65 | 46 | 62 | 25 | 35 | 18 | 7.3 | 82 |
| 90 | 64 | 44 | 60 | 25 | 38 | 18 | 7.2 | 83 |
| 90 | 63 | 42 | 60 | 25 | 36 | 18 | 6.6 | 84 |
| 91 | 63 | 42 | 60 | 25 | 35 | 18 | 6.5 | 85 |
| 91 | 63 | 43 | 58 | 27 | 31 | 18 | 6.3 | 86 |
| 91 | 66 | 44 | 59 | 27 | 29 | 17 | 6.0 | 87 |
| 91 | 67 | 45 | 59 | 26 | . | 16 | 5.8 | 88 |
| 91 | 69 | 46 | 62 | 25 | . | 16 | 5.9 | 89 |
| 91 | 70 | 47 | 65 | 27 | . | 15 | . | 1990 |

[b] South-West Asia excluding Turkey.

[c] Northern sub-Saharan Africa.

### 3.2. *The journey extended to South-West Asia and Northern Africa*

The remainder of Table 2-7 concerns countries on Europe's periphery and beyond. Turkey's GDP ratios (column 14) are virtually constant around 25 percent. This is about the same level as that of Portugal (column 12) in 1950, but the latter country showed substantial improvements over time. In column 15 we consider South-West Asia excluding Turkey, consisting of five countries: Iran, Iraq, Israel, Jordan. Syria.[3] The GDP ratios of this region increase from less than 40 percent in the early 1960s to about 50 percent in the mid-1970s, after which they decline to less than 30 percent in 1987 (close to the Turkish value). The market for oil products has a dominant influence on this region.

In columns 16 and 17 we cross the Mediterranean Sea and move to North Africa and Northern sub-Saharan Africa. North Africa consists of four countries: Algeria, Egypt, Morocco, Tunisia. (No data are available for Libya.) Its GDP ratios remain virtually constant at the 15 percent level from 1960 to 1990 and are hence much lower than anywhere in Europe, Turkey or South-West Asia. Northern sub-Saharan Africa consists of five countries: Chad, Mali, Mauritania, Niger, Sudan. The GDP ratios of this region are even lower than those of North Africa and they are declining, from about 9 percent in the early 1970s to less than 6 percent in the late 1980s. This is a reflection of a more general phenomenon that we will find repeatedly in the journeys described in this section: Affluence tends to decline when we move toward the Equator.

### 3.3. *From South Africa in northern direction*

In Table 2-8 we consider South Africa, which is Africa's economic powerhouse, together with its five Northern neighbors as well as the four countries North of these neighbors. Column 2 shows that South Africa's GDP per capita was subject to an increasing trend, from less than 2000 in the early 1950s to more than 3500 in the early 1980s, after which there was a decline.

The entries in all other columns of Table 2-8 are GDP ratios (relative to the South African values in column 2). As far as South Africa's immediate neighbors are concerned (columns 3 to 7), some are doing relatively well (Namibia and Swaziland); in one case (Botswana) there is a considerable improvement in the late 1980s; and in two cases (Zimbabwe and Mozambique) there is stagnancy relative to South Africa or even a substantial decline. The last column of the table refers to the four-country region farther North (and closer to the Equator), consisting of Angola, Malawi, Tanzania and Zambia. The numbers in that column show that this region is in serious trouble.

[3] Data for all five countries are available only for the period 1960–1987. For several other countries in this region (such as Kuwait, Lebanon and Saudi Arabia) data are either available for even shorter periods or not at all.

*Table 2-8.* GDP per capita in Southern Africa[a]

| Year (1) | South Africa (2) | Neighbors of South Africa: Namibia (3) | Botswana (4) | Zimbabwe (5) | Swaziland (6) | Mozambique (7) | Farther north[b] (8) |
|---|---|---|---|---|---|---|---|
| 1950 | 1865 | . | . | . | . | . | . |
| 51 | 1904 | . | . | . | . | . | . |
| 52 | 1837 | . | . | . | . | . | . |
| 53 | 1956 | . | . | . | . | . | . |
| 54 | 2020 | . | . | 44 | . | . | . |
| 55 | 2046 | . | . | 47 | . | . | . |
| 56 | 2087 | . | . | 50 | . | . | . |
| 57 | 2134 | . | . | 50 | . | . | . |
| 58 | 2130 | . | . | 49 | . | . | . |
| 59 | 2133 | . | . | 47 | . | . | . |
| 1960 | 2109 | 84 | 26 | 47 | 58 | 54 | 26 |
| 61 | 2133 | 83 | 27 | 47 | 72 | 53 | 26 |
| 62 | 2208 | 88 | 27 | 42 | 74 | 54 | 25 |
| 63 | 2332 | 88 | 26 | 38 | 71 | 53 | 24 |
| 64 | 2450 | 90 | 26 | 37 | 73 | 50 | 23 |
| 65 | 2522 | 91 | 24 | 37 | 67 | 49 | 25 |
| 66 | 2587 | 91 | 23 | 37 | 68 | 48 | 24 |
| 67 | 2687 | 87 | 27 | 37 | 62 | 50 | 24 |
| 68 | 2756 | 86 | 29 | 35 | 65 | 51 | 24 |
| 69 | 2896 | 84 | 29 | 35 | 73 | 51 | 23 |
| 1970 | 3146 | 83 | 27 | 34 | 77 | 46 | 21 |
| 71 | 3244 | 80 | 28 | 35 | 73 | 47 | 21 |
| 72 | 3180 | 87 | 34 | 39 | 80 | 49 | 22 |
| 73 | 3315 | 86 | 38 | 37 | 76 | 49 | 21 |
| 74 | 3529 | 88 | 40 | 37 | 63 | 39 | 20 |
| 75 | 3490 | 82 | 38 | 37 | 71 | 33 | 19 |
| 76 | 3456 | 87 | 40 | 34 | 69 | 31 | 18 |
| 77 | 3285 | 98 | 40 | 34 | 78 | 33 | 18 |
| 78 | 3309 | 102 | 45 | 35 | 89 | 32 | 19 |
| 79 | 3339 | 104 | 49 | 35 | 96 | 32 | 18 |
| 1980 | 3512 | 69 | 53 | 33 | 86 | 26 | 17 |
| 81 | 3700 | 70 | 51 | 33 | 86 | 25 | 15 |
| 82 | 3602 | 68 | 53 | 35 | 75 | 24 | 16 |
| 83 | 3399 | 66 | 54 | 39 | 68 | 25 | 15 |
| 84 | 3541 | 62 | 54 | 33 | 69 | 23 | 15 |
| 85 | 3354 | 64 | 67 | 35 | 64 | 21 | 16 |
| 86 | 3299 | 64 | 63 | 36 | 61 | 22 | 17 |
| 87 | 3288 | 66 | 65 | 37 | 61 | 21 | 17 |
| 88 | 3372 | 64 | 72 | 36 | 62 | 21 | 17 |
| 89 | 3316 | 62 | 97 | 39 | 66 | 23 | . |
| 1990 | 3191 | . | . | 40 | . | 23 | . |

[a] The entries in column 2 are in 1985 international prices; those in all other columns express the per capita GDP as a percentage of the South Africa value (column 2) in the same year.
[b] The four-country region consisting of Angola, Malawi, Tanzania and Zambia.

### 3.4. *Two journeys in the Americas*

In the left half of Table 2-9 we compare the United States with Mexico and Central America. Column 2 (taken from Table 2-2) shows that the U.S. per capita GDP more than doubled from 1950 to 1990. The Mexican GDP ratio (relative to USA) increased from 25 percent in 1950 to 40 percent in 1980, after which it declined to less than 30 percent. The GDP ratios of Central America (Costa Rica, El Salvador, Guatemala, Honduras, Nicaragua, Panama) were virtually constant at about 15 percent, but they declined somewhat in the 1980s.

The right half of Table 2-9 compares the Southern cone of South America (Argentina, Chile, Uruguay) with Brazil and the three-country region West of Brazil (Bolivia, Paraguay, Peru). The Southern cone's GDP per capita increased form about 3000 in 1950 to 4500 in 1980, after which it declined to less than 4000. Brazil's GDP ratio (relative to the Southern cone) was subject to a sizeable upward trend, from about 40 percent in the early 1950s to more than 100 percent in the second half of the 1980s. The development of the GDP ratio of the region West of Brazil was similar to that of Brazil until 1970, but its development after 1970 was not characterized by Brazil's success.

### 3.5. *From south to north in the Western Pacific*

Our fifth journey takes us to the non-Communist countries in the Western Pacific Rim as well as some island nations in the Western Pacific Ocean. We shall find it convenient to take Australia and New Zealand as a starting point. To a large extent, these two countries are comparable with the USA and Canada: First, all four are New World countries. Second, all four are predominantly populated by English-speaking whites living in mostly temperate zones. (Outback Australia and Arctic Canada are not exactly temperate, but very few people are living there.) Third, all four have per capita incomes that are either at or near the top in their own Hemisphere (USA and Canada in the Northern Hemisphere, Australia and New Zealand in the Southern Hemisphere).

Column 2 of Table 2-10 gives the per capita GDP of the two-country region (Australia plus New Zealand). It shows an upward trend from less than 7000 in the early 1950s to about 14000 in the late 1980s. The other columns of the table deal with individual countries, starting with New Zealand and Australia (columns 3 and 4) and then moving North toward the Equator and beyond. The entries in these columns are all GDP ratios relative to the two-country region in column 2.

It follows from columns 3 and 4 that, apart form the early 1960s, Australia was consistently better-off than New Zealand. Next, when moving toward the Equator in columns 5 to 9, we find that the GDP ratios drop substantially. The ratios of Fiji fluctuate around one-quarter (25 percent) and those of Western Samoa and the Solomon Islands are even smaller, while those of

*Table 2-9.* GDP per capita in the Americas

| | North and Middle America[a] | | | South America[b] | | |
|---|---|---|---|---|---|---|
| Year (1) | USA (2) | Mexico (3) | Central America (4) | Southern cone (5) | Brazil (6) | West-of-Brazil (7) |
| 1950 | 8625 | 25 | 15 | 2921 | 43 | 47 |
| 51 | 8987 | 26 | 14 | 3019 | 41 | 49 |
| 52 | 8998 | 26 | 15 | 2862 | 47 | 52 |
| 53 | 9226 | 24 | 15 | 2919 | 46 | 49 |
| 54 | 9006 | 26 | 15 | 3002 | 48 | 50 |
| 55 | 9593 | 26 | 14 | 3119 | 48 | 50 |
| 56 | 9584 | 27 | 15 | 3076 | 48 | 51 |
| 57 | 9530 | 28 | 15 | 3212 | 49 | 49 |
| 58 | 9278 | 29 | 16 | 3302 | 50 | 47 |
| 59 | 9718 | 28 | 15 | 3086 | 55 | 49 |
| 1960 | 9776 | 29 | 15 | 3237 | 54 | 51 |
| 61 | 9835 | 29 | 15 | 3408 | 54 | 51 |
| 62 | 10234 | 28 | 15 | 3309 | 57 | 56 |
| 63 | 10514 | 28 | 16 | 3220 | 58 | 59 |
| 64 | 10928 | 30 | 15 | 3423 | 54 | 57 |
| 65 | 11492 | 29 | 15 | 3585 | 51 | 56 |
| 66 | 11999 | 29 | 15 | 3624 | 52 | 59 |
| 67 | 12160 | 29 | 15 | 3647 | 53 | 59 |
| 68 | 12555 | 30 | 15 | 3723 | 57 | 56 |
| 69 | 12806 | 30 | 15 | 3904 | 56 | 55 |
| 1970 | 12725 | 31 | 15 | 4017 | 60 | 57 |
| 71 | 13041 | 31 | 15 | 4172 | 63 | 56 |
| 72 | 13632 | 30 | 15 | 4164 | 69 | 56 |
| 73 | 14226 | 31 | 15 | 4165 | 77 | 58 |
| 74 | 13909 | 32 | 16 | 4256 | 80 | 60 |
| 75 | 13479 | 34 | 16 | 4032 | 86 | 63 |
| 76 | 14087 | 33 | 16 | 3941 | 95 | 65 |
| 77 | 14655 | 31 | 16 | 4143 | 92 | 61 |
| 78 | 15303 | 32 | 16 | 4101 | 94 | 60 |
| 79 | 15408 | 34 | 15 | 4399 | 92 | 57 |
| 1980 | 15097 | 38 | 15 | 4537 | 94 | 58 |
| 81 | 15339 | 40 | 15 | 4381 | 90 | 62 |
| 82 | 14612 | 38 | 15 | 3859 | 101 | 68 |
| 83 | 15039 | 34 | 14 | 3818 | 97 | 60 |
| 84 | 16154 | 32 | 13 | 3894 | 97 | 59 |
| 85 | 16559 | 32 | 12 | 3704 | 107 | 62 |
| 86 | 16885 | 29 | 12 | 3882 | 108 | 62 |
| 87 | 17332 | 28 | 12 | 3984 | 106 | 63 |
| 88 | 17975 | 28 | . | 3870 | 106 | 60 |
| 89 | 18354 | 28 | . | 3771 | 110 | 55 |
| 1990 | 18399 | 29 | . | 3692 | 106 | 53 |

[a] The entries in column 2 are in 1985 international prices; those in columns 3 and 4 express the per capita GDP as a percentage of the U.S. value (column 2) in the same year.
[b] The entries in column 5 are in 1985 international prices; those in columns 6 and 7 express the per capita GDP as a percentage of the Southern cone value (column 5) in the same year.

*Table 2-10.* GDPs per capita in the Western Pacific, 1950–1990[a]

| Year (1) | Australia + N. Zealand (2) | New Zealand (3) | Australia (4) | Fiji (5) | Western Samoa (6) | Solomon Islands (7) | Papua N. Guinea (8) | Indonesia (9) |
|---|---|---|---|---|---|---|---|---|
| 1950 | 6743 | 98 | 100 | . | . | . | . | . |
| 51 | 6613 | 94 | 101 | . | . | . | . | . |
| 52 | 6094 | 99 | 100 | . | . | . | . | . |
| 53 | 6611 | 91 | 102 | . | . | . | . | . |
| 54 | 7078 | 96 | 101 | . | . | . | . | . |
| 55 | 7222 | 95 | 101 | . | . | . | . | . |
| 56 | 7076 | 95 | 101 | . | . | . | . | . |
| 57 | 7108 | 98 | 100 | . | . | . | . | . |
| 58 | 7374 | 93 | 102 | . | . | . | . | . |
| 59 | 7657 | 92 | 102 | . | . | . | . | . |
| 1960 | 7887 | 100 | 100 | 26 | . | . | 14 | 7.9 |
| 61 | 7743 | 104 | 99 | 27 | . | . | 16 | 8.4 |
| 62 | 8093 | 100 | 100 | 25 | . | . | 16 | 7.9 |
| 63 | 8458 | 99 | 100 | 26 | . | . | 16 | 7.1 |
| 64 | 8916 | 97 | 101 | 26 | . | . | 17 | 6.8 |
| 65 | 8962 | 100 | 100 | 23 | . | . | 17 | 6.6 |
| 66 | 9245 | 98 | 100 | 22 | . | . | 18 | 6.5 |
| 67 | 9345 | 93 | 102 | 23 | . | . | 17 | 6.5 |
| 68 | 9929 | 86 | 103 | 22 | . | . | 17 | 6.3 |
| 69 | 10283 | 88 | 103 | 22 | . | . | 18 | 6.5 |
| 1970 | 10629 | 88 | 103 | 24 | . | . | 16 | 6.6 |
| 71 | 10794 | 90 | 102 | 25 | . | . | 17 | 6.7 |
| 72 | 11049 | 90 | 102 | 25 | . | . | 16 | 6.8 |
| 73 | 11491 | 93 | 102 | 27 | . | . | 15 | 7.1 |
| 74 | 11452 | 97 | 101 | 28 | . | . | 15 | 7.7 |
| 75 | 11407 | 92 | 102 | 28 | . | . | 15 | 8.2 |
| 76 | 11632 | 91 | 102 | 28 | . | . | 14 | 8.3 |
| 77 | 11429 | 87 | 103 | 29 | . | . | 14 | 8.9 |
| 78 | 11858 | 84 | 104 | 28 | . | . | 14 | 9.3 |
| 79 | 11966 | 86 | 103 | 31 | 17 | . | 14 | 9.8 |
| 1980 | 12209 | 84 | 103 | 29 | 14 | 12 | 14 | 10.3 |
| 81 | 12466 | 86 | 103 | 30 | 13 | 12 | 13 | 11.7 |
| 82 | 11911 | 90 | 102 | 28 | 13 | 11 | 13 | 12.3 |
| 83 | 12487 | 87 | 103 | 26 | 12 | 12 | 12 | 12.4 |
| 84 | 12998 | 87 | 103 | 26 | 12 | 12 | 12 | 12.2 |
| 85 | 13258 | 85 | 103 | 24 | 12 | 11 | 11 | 12.3 |
| 86 | 13356 | 86 | 103 | 24 | 13 | 12 | 11 | 12.4 |
| 87 | 13731 | 84 | 103 | 22 | 13 | 12 | 11 | 12.2 |
| 88 | 14131 | 81 | 104 | 22 | 12 | 13 | 11 | 12.0 |
| 89 | 14395 | 82 | 104 | 25 | 12 | . | 10 | 12.5 |
| 1990 | 13845 | 83 | 103 | 27 | 12 | . | 10 | 14.0 |

[a] The entries in column 2 are in 1985 international prices; those in all other columns express the per capita GDP as a percentage of the value in column 2 in the same year.

| Singapore (10) | Malaysia (11) | Thailand (12) | Philippines (13) | Hong Kong (14) | Taiwan (15) | Japan (16) | South Korea (17) | Year (18) |
|---|---|---|---|---|---|---|---|---|
| . | . | 13 | 11 | . | . | 22 | . | 1950 |
| . | . | 12 | 12 | . | 14 | 25 | . | 51 |
| . | . | 13 | 14 | . | 17 | 30 | . | 52 |
| . | . | 11 | 14 | . | 17 | 29 | 12 | 53 |
| . | . | 11 | 13 | . | 17 | 28 | 12 | 54 |
| . | 18 | 10 | 14 | . | 17 | 29 | 12 | 55 |
| . | 18 | 10 | 15 | . | 18 | 32 | 13 | 56 |
| . | 18 | 11 | 14 | . | 18 | 34 | 13 | 57 |
| . | 17 | 11 | 14 | . | 18 | 34 | 13 | 58 |
| . | 17 | 11 | 14 | . | 18 | 35 | 12 | 59 |
| 22 | 18 | 12 | 14 | 28 | 18 | 38 | 12 | 1960 |
| 23 | 19 | 12 | 15 | 30 | 18 | 44 | 12 | 61 |
| 23 | 19 | 12 | 15 | 31 | 18 | 45 | 12 | 62 |
| 23 | 18 | 12 | 14 | 34 | 18 | 47 | 12 | 63 |
| 21 | 18 | 12 | 14 | 35 | 19 | 50 | 11 | 64 |
| 22 | 18 | 13 | 14 | 39 | 20 | 51 | 12 | 65 |
| 22 | 18 | 13 | 13 | 40 | 20 | 55 | 13 | 66 |
| 24 | 18 | 13 | 14 | 40 | 22 | 59 | 13 | 67 |
| 25 | 18 | 13 | 13 | 39 | 21 | 63 | 14 | 68 |
| 28 | 17 | 13 | 13 | 41 | 21 | 67 | 14 | 69 |
| 30 | 20 | 14 | 13 | 42 | 22 | 71 | 16 | 1970 |
| 32 | 20 | 14 | 13 | 44 | 24 | 71 | 17 | 71 |
| 35 | 21 | 14 | 13 | 47 | 26 | 74 | 17 | 72 |
| 39 | 22 | 14 | 13 | 50 | 27 | 76 | 18 | 73 |
| 40 | 24 | 14 | 14 | 49 | 28 | 74 | 20 | 74 |
| 44 | 23 | 15 | 14 | 49 | 29 | 75 | 20 | 75 |
| 45 | 24 | 15 | 14 | 54 | 31 | 76 | 22 | 76 |
| 49 | 26 | 16 | 15 | 61 | 34 | 80 | 25 | 77 |
| 50 | 27 | 17 | 15 | 65 | 36 | 81 | 26 | 78 |
| 54 | 29 | 18 | 15 | 67 | 38 | 83 | 28 | 79 |
| 57 | 31 | 18 | 15 | 72 | 40 | 84 | 26 | 1980 |
| 59 | 32 | 18 | 15 | 76 | 40 | 85 | 26 | 81 |
| 65 | 35 | 18 | 16 | 81 | 42 | 91 | 29 | 82 |
| 65 | 34 | 19 | 15 | 81 | 42 | 88 | 30 | 83 |
| 66 | 34 | 19 | 13 | 82 | 43 | 88 | 31 | 84 |
| 61 | 31 | 18 | 11 | 80 | 44 | 91 | 32 | 85 |
| 61 | 28 | 18 | 11 | 87 | 47 | 92 | 35 | 86 |
| 64 | 27 | 19 | 12 | 95 | 51 | 93 | 37 | 87 |
| 68 | 29 | 21 | 12 | 98 | 54 | 95 | 40 | 88 |
| 71 | 31 | 22 | 12 | 97 | 57 | 98 | 43 | 89 |
| 79 | 35 | 26 | 13 | 104 | 61 | 107 | . | 1990 |

Papua New Guinea tend to decline over time. Evidently, in none of these cases is there a tendency toward elimination of the GDP gap between them and the two-country region in column 2. We reach the Equator in column 9 (Indonesia), where the GDP ratios take the lowest values (less than 10 percent), at least until the early 1980s.

From column 10 onward we move away from the Equator in Northern direction, and we find that during this journey the GDP ratios tend to rise, although there are exceptions. Note the rapid increase of Singapore's ratios over time (column 10), from less than 25 percent in the early 1960s until almost 80 percent in 1990. The figures for Malaysia are not much better than those of Papua New Guinea during the 1960s (columns 11 and 8), but the Malaysian ratios are much more promising in the 1980s. Thailand and the Philippines (columns 12 and 13) have comparable GDP ratios until about 1980 when Thailand moves ahead. Hong Kong is similar to Singapore, and so is Taiwan (but Taiwan is poorer than the city-states in each year). Japan grew fast relative to the two-country region (columns 16 and 2) since 1960. In fact, Japan and Hong Kong are the only two whose per capita GDP exceeded the Australian value in 1990. South Korea also moved ahead, but it is still well below Japan's level.

## 4. The Equatorial Grand Canyon

In the two previous sections we considered either groups of countries (regions) or regions plus individual countries. In this section we shall consider individual countries only.

### 4.1. *Preliminaries*

The major conclusions to be drawn from the five journeys of Section 3 is that affluence tends to decline when we move toward the Equator from the temperate zones in either the Northern or the Southern Hemisphere. Needless to say, this tendency is not without exceptions nor is it constant over time (great civilizations originated near the Equator). Nevertheless, its existence as a tendency in the non-Communist world in the last several decades cannot be denied. It is tempting to compare this with some of the writings of Ellsworth Huntington and Arnold Toynbee, but we shall resist this temptation. Instead, we shall attempt to formulate a simple model for per capita GDP based on the country's latitude. This model is not a formal statistical model in the sense that it provides a specification of the statistical structure of the error term. Rather, we shall want to compare the fit of our model with that of an even simpler model which denies the effect of latitude.

Recall that we defined two regions in high-latitude zones and five in low-latitude zones in Section 2.1 (and that the former two are more affluent than the latter five). We should mention here that latitudes also play a prominent role in the following five-zone classification which has been used in geography for a long time. First, there is the *torrid zone*, located between the Tropic of Cancer and the Tropic of Capricorn. Second and third, there are the *Northern temperate zone* (from the Tropic of Cancer to the Arctic Circle) and the *Southern temperate zone* (from the Tropic of Capricorn to the Antarctic Circle). Finally, there are two *frigid zones* (North of the Arctic Circle and South of the Antarctic Circle), but these will play no role in our analysis.

For the discussion which follows in Section 4.3 it is important to note that 45 degrees North is the *mid-circle* of the Northern temperate zone (it is also the mid-circle of the Northern Hemisphere); 45 degrees South has a similar property. See Sanders (1991) for an instructive exposition of climatic zones which goes beyond what is presented here.

### 4.2. *The latitude of a country*

Each country has a northernmost and a southernmost latitude. For example, the United States stretches from northernmost Alaska (about 71 degrees North) to southernmost Hawaii (about 19 degrees North). These two extremes can be viewed as defining the range of the country's latitude distribution. For our purpose it is more convenient to use one single latitude value. One possibility is the average of the extremes, or the mid-range. For the U.S. this would be about 45 degrees North, which happens to be the latitude of Minneapolis. The question to be asked is whether more attractive single-value measures can be found.

One candidate is the latitude of the country's population center of gravity. This center is the mean of the population distribution. A problem with this choice is the fact that the population center of gravity may not be on land when the country consists (partly or wholly) of islands. Also, this center may be located in a different country. For example, Pakistan's population center of gravity was located in India prior to the independence of Bangladesh. (The mid-range has of course the same problems.)

We can avoid these problems by defining, as we shall do in this section, the latitude of a country as the latitude of its most populous city. The location of this city represents the mode of the population distribution. Another choice would be the latitude of the country's capital. Indeed, Theil and Finke (1983), when using the distance from the Equator as an instrumental variable for income in a system of cross-country demand equations, defined this distance in terms of the latitude of the country's capital. However, this gives problems when the country assigns the capital function to more than one city, as is the case for South Africa with Cape Town as legislative capital and Pretoria as administrative capital. (No such problem arose in the 30-country sample used by Theil and Finke.)

### 4.3. *A piecewise linear latitude model*

We start with the year 1985, for which the Summers-Heston (1993) data set covers the largest number (140) of non-Communist countries. However, for the purpose of the latitude model to be developed below we shall delete the two city-states (Hong Kong and Singapore). The reason is that such a state has a "truncated" economy in the sense that its agricultural sector is artificially small compared with those of surrounding countries. (Given the relatively small populations of these two states, it is unlikely that the model is greatly affected by their inclusion or exclusion, but it is statistically unwise to include known outliers.)

Each of the remaining 138 countries has its latitude $L_i$, measured in degrees and defined here (as stated above) as the latitude of its most populous city. We proceed to introduce four regions for the purpose of our latitude model. First, there is the region centered around the Equator, $C_k = (-k, k)$, where $k$ is a number of degrees to be fitted ($-k$ stands for $k$ degrees South). Next are two regions North and South of the Central region, $N_k = (k, 45)$ and $S_k = (-45, -k)$ where 45 degrees (North or South) is the mid-circle mentioned at the end of Section 4.1. Finally, there is the region $F = (45, 65)$ North of $N_k$. All 138 countries are located in one of these four regions for any value of $k$, $0 < k < 45$. There are no countries whose most populous city is located in the Southern counterpart of $F$. In the Northern Hemisphere we have Iceland and Finland whose most populous cities (Reykjavik and Helsinki) are between 60 and 65 degrees North; all 136 other countries have a most populous city below 60 degrees North and above 40 degrees South.

We write $R_i$ for the GDP ratio of country $i$ relative to the U.S.: the per capita GDP of country $i$ divided by that of the U.S.[4] Our next objective is to formulate the prediction $\hat{R}_i$ implied by the latitude model. Keeping our desire for simplicity in mind, we define $\hat{R}_i$ for all countries in $C_k$ as that region's GDP ratio,

$$\hat{R}_i = \overline{R}_k \quad \text{if} \quad i \in C_k$$

where

$$\overline{R}_k = \Big(\sum_{j \in C_k} p_j R_j\Big) \Big/ \Big(\sum_{j \in C_k} p_j\Big)$$

with $p_j$ defined as the population share of country $j$ ($p_1 + \ldots + p_{138} = 1$). Similarly, the model predicts that all countries in $F$ have a GDP ratio equal to the unit level (that is, the U.S. level):

$$\hat{R}_i = 1 \quad \text{if} \quad i \in F$$

[4] These are GDP ratios similar to those of columns 3 and 4 of Table 2-9 (except that they are not expressed as percentages). Two countries (Qatar and United Arab Emirates) have GDP ratios exceeding 1 in 1985, but his does not affect our analysis.

For $N_k$ and $S_k$ the prediction is a linear function of the latitude $L_i$. Thus, $\hat{R}_i$ for country $i$ in these two regions is

$$\hat{R}_i = \overline{R}_k + (1 - \overline{R}_k)(L_i - k)/(45 - k) \quad \text{if} \quad i \in N_k$$

$$\hat{R}_i = 1 - (1 - \overline{R}_k)(45 + L_i)/(45 - k) \quad \text{if} \quad i \in S_k$$

It may be verified (by substituting $L_i = \pm k$ and $L_i = \pm 45$ in the above two equations) that $\hat{R}_i$ is a continuous function of $L_i$ in the entire range, $-45 < L_i < 65$.

### 4.4. *The Equatorial Grand Canyon in 1985*

In the next paragraph we shall argue that the appropriate criterion is the population-weighted mean square error,

$$V_k = \sum_{i=1}^{138} p_i(\hat{R}_i - R_i)^2$$

which is a function of $k$ (as the notation $V_k$ indicates). Table 2-11 shows the value of $V_k$ for selected values of $k$; it indicates that $V_k$ is minimized at $k$ = 30 degrees and the associated $\overline{R}_{30}$ is 0.101. An interesting way of visualizing this result is by means of a *canyon* centered around the Equator whose bottom is $C_{30} = (-30, 30)$, which exceeds the torrid zone (see Section 4.1) by almost 30 percent. Also, this bottom is just 10 percent above Absolute Zero ($\overline{R}_{30} \approx 0.1$).[5] The canyon is surrounded by two slopes, the North Slope $N_{30}$ and the South Slope $S_{30}$, and North of the North Slope is the Northern Plateau $F$. In terms of populations, the countries that figure prominently at the bottom are India (765 m), Indonesia (163 m) and Brazil (136 m), followed by Pakistan, Bangladesh and Nigeria (all between 95 and 100 m). The most

*Table 2-11.* The minimization in 1985

| $k$ | $V_k$ | $k$ | $V_k$ |
|---|---|---|---|
| 5 degrees | 0.12007 | 29 | 0.03131 |
| 10 | 0.08868 | 30 | 0.03128 |
| 15 | 0.06523 | 31 | 0.03172 |
| 20 | 0.04509 | 32 | 0.03277 |
| 25 | 0.03404 | 33 | 0.03472 |
| 26 | 0.03316 | 34 | 0.03751 |
| 27 | 0.03234 | 35 | 0.04134 |
| 28 | 0.03168 | 40 | 0.07111 |

[5] If the reader insists, he (or she) can relate this Absolute Zero to the river that caused the canyon. This river, which may be called the E-river, coincides with the Equator. It is the longest river in the world; in fact, its length is just over 40,000 kilometers. The bottom of the E-river coincides with Absolute Zero.

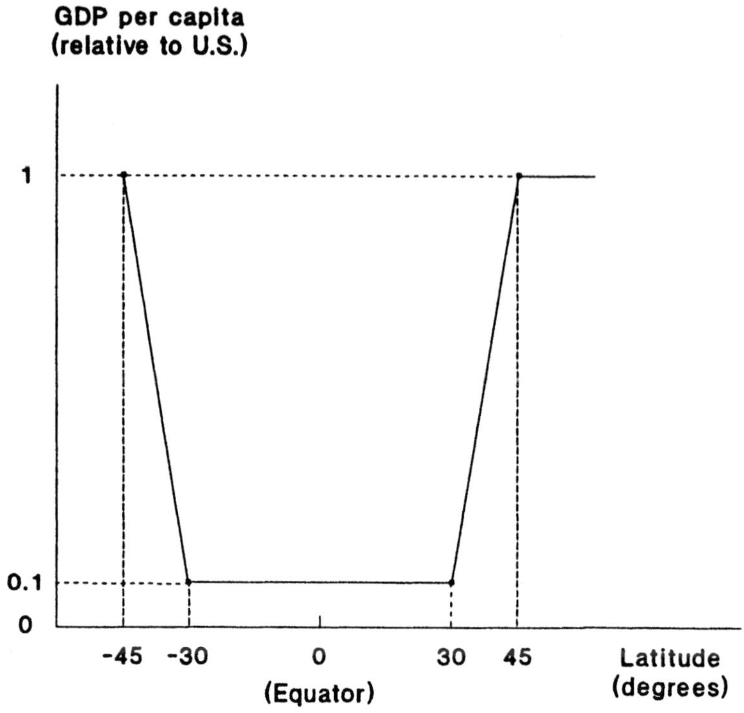


*Figure 2-3.* The Equatorial Grand Canyon in 1985.

prominent country at or near the Northern Plateau is the United States (239 m), while Japan (121 m) figures prominently on the North Slope. The canyon is illustrated in Figure 2-3.

To put these results into proper perspective we should compare the latitude model with a model that denies the effect of latitude. If latitude does not matter, and given that latitude is the only factor considered here, each country's GDP ratio equals the world's GDP ratio apart from an unpredictable discrepancy. The world's GDP ratio equals the population-weighted mean of the 138 GDP ratios:

$$\overline{R} = \sum_{i=1}^{138} p_i R_i$$

Where $\overline{R}$ is used to predict each $R_i$, the mean square error is the population-weighted variance of the 138 GDP ratios, to be called the *GDP variance*:

$$V = \sum_{i=1}^{138} p_i (R_i - \overline{R})^2$$

A comparison of the formulas for $V$ and $V_k$ shows that the appropriate criterion for the fit of our latitude model is indeed the population-weighted mean square error $V_k$.

For our 1985 data we obtain

$$\overline{R} = 0.272, \qquad V = 0.0971$$

On comparing the value of $V$ with the minimum shown in Table 2-11 we conclude that our one-parameter canyon model accounts for about 68 percent of the variance of the per capita GDPs.

## 4.5. *Alternative models*

The reader is perhaps surprised that our latitude model consists of four straight-line segments. Isn't it more natural to use a smoother version? The answer is that an effort was made to formulate a smooth model. When we turn the canyon *upside down*, we find that it takes a bell-shaped form, or at least a straight-line approximation to such a form. Accordingly, we considered density functions of various symmetric distributions centered around the Equator.

More specifically, "upside down" means that we replace $R_i$ by $S_i = 1 - R_i$, to be called the *shortfall* of country $i$ relative to the U.S.: $S_i$ equals the excess of the U.S. per capita GDP over that of country $i$, measured as a fraction of the U.S. value. We considered a shortfall function of latitude, $S(L)$, which is proportional to the density of a symmetric Beta distribution over the interval from the Antarctic Circle to the Arctic Circle. Thus we have

$$S(L) = S_0(1 - L^2)^\beta$$

where $L = 1$ stands for the Arctic Circle, $L = 0$ for the Equator, and $L = -1$ for the Antarctic Circle. (Hence $L$ is not measured in degrees in this section.) The Beta model has two parameters: $\beta \geq 0$ and $S_0$ which is the shortfall at the Equator.

For an individual country we have $S_i = S(L_i) + e_i$, where $e_i$ is a residual. Next we minimize $\sum_i p_i e_i^2$ as in the previous section. Surprisingly, this yields a value of $S_0$ exceeding 1 in 1985, implying a negative GDP at the Equator, which is unacceptable. Also, the population-weighted mean square error of the Beta model is larger (almost 20 percent) than that of the canyon model in spite of the fact that it adjusts more parameters.

We suspected that India was the problem. To verify this suspicion we conducted a simple experiment by subtracting 100 million from India's population, leaving all other 1985 population and per capita GDP data (and all latitudes) unchanged, and then subtracting 200 million, and so on. This does indeed reduce the minimizing value of $S_0$; its value drops below 1 when India's population is reduced by 500 million (so that it becomes 265 m).

We mention this result mainly because readers may want to conduct their own experiments and select their own curves (Beta or otherwise). If such a curve has a unique extremum at the Equator (a maximum shortfall or a minimum per capita GDP), there is the risk that the curve violates the positivity constraint on GDP at the Equator. The canyon solution that we adopted avoids this problem by equating $\hat{R}_i$ to $\overline{R}_k > 0$ for all $i \in C_k$. An unusual aspect of the data used here is the vast difference of the populations of the countries covered (ranging from India's 765 m to Seychelles' 65,000 in 1985).

4.6. *Binary countries*

When we extend the canyon model to years before and after 1985, we must face the fact that the Summers-Heston data cover different sets of countries in different years. We shall solve this problem by applying the canyon model to pairs of successive years, to be written $(t-1, t)$, starting with 1950–51, and using only *binary countries*; that is, countries for which data are available in both $t-1$ and $t$.

The number of binary countries, written $N_t$ for $(t-1, t)$, changes considerably over time. As column 2 of Table 2-12 shows, we have $N_t = 59$ for $t = 1951$ (1950–51), $N_t = 126$ for $t = 1985$ (1984–85), and $N_t = 132$ for $t = 1986$ (1985–86). To understand the latter two values, recall from Section 4.3 that there are 138 countries in 1985. There are six countries missing in 1986 that were included in 1985 (Belize, Bhutan, Dominica, St. Lucia, St. Vincennes/Grenadines, Tonga), implying $N_t = 138 - 6 = 132$ for $t = 1986$ (1985–86). These six countries are also missing in 1984, as well as another six (all oil states in the Arabian Peninsula: Bahrain, Kuwait, Oman, Qatar, Saudi Arabia, United Arab Emirates), implying $N_t = 126$ for $t = 1985$ (1984–85). These oil states were all added to the data set in 1985 for the first time.

We write $R_{it}$ for the GDP ratio of country $i$ in year $t$: the GDP per capita of $i$ in $t$ divided by the U.S. value in that year. In columns 3 and 4 of Table 2-12 we consider the world GDP ratio, $\overline{R}$, for the pair $(t-1, t)$. In column 4 this is computed for year $t$ as the sum of $p_{it}R_{it}$ and in column 3 for $t-1$ as the sum of $p_{i,t-1}R_{i,t-1}$ (both sums are over the $N_t$ values of $i$), where $p_{it}$ and $p_{i,t-1}$ are population shares. Thus, the first row of the table shows that in the comparison of 1950 and 1951, $\overline{R}$ in 1950 equals 0.295 (that is, gross world product per capita in 1950 equals 29.5 percent of the U.S. GDP per capita in 1950), and that this $\overline{R}$ went down slightly (to 0.290) in 1951. The numbers in columns 3 and 4 are rather stable, with $\overline{R}$'s between 0.27 and 0.31. This stability is the result of our dividing the per capita GDPs by the U.S. value in the same year.

Also note that in most cases the entry in column 4 in any row is equal to that in column 3 in the next row. However, there are exceptions which are due to a change in the set of binary countries. For example, the row for 1984–85 shows that $\overline{R}$ in 1985 equals 0.269 (column 4), but the next row yields $\overline{R} = 0.272$ for that year (column 3). This amounts to a discontinuity which results from the addition (noted earlier in this section) of the six oil states in 1985–86. Such discontinuities occur elsewhere in Table 2-12 also.

Columns 5 and 6 deal with the GDP variance $V$. The computation of the two values of $V$ for the pair $(t-1, t)$ is analogous to that of $\overline{R}$ in columns 3

*Table 2-12.* The Canyon model in four decades

| Years | | $1000\overline{R}$ | | $10{,}000V$ | | $10{,}000V_k$ | | $k$ | | $1000\overline{R}_k$ | |
|---|---|---|---|---|---|---|---|---|---|---|---|
| $(t-1, t)$ | $N_t$ | $t-1$ | $t$ | $t-1$ | $t$ | $t-1$ | $t$ | $t-1$ | $t$ | $t-1$ | $t$ |
| (1) | (2) | (3) | (4) | (5) | (6) | (7) | (8) | (9) | (10) | (11) | (12) |
| 1950–51 | 59 | 295 | 290 | 980 | 955 | 756 | 720 | 32.8 | 32.7 | 89 | 88 |
| 51–52 | 61 | 290 | 294 | 966 | 964 | 720 | 683 | 32.6 | 32.6 | 87 | 89 |
| 52–53 | 61 | 294 | 288 | 964 | 952 | 683 | 652 | 32.6 | 32.5 | 89 | 88 |
| 53–54 | 65 | 291 | 301 | 958 | 973 | 673 | 619 | 32.9 | 32.7 | 88 | 95 |
| 54–55 | 69 | 301 | 290 | 976 | 954 | 619 | 599 | 32.7 | 32.7 | 95 | 91 |
| 55–56 | 74 | 294 | 299 | 959 | 973 | 602 | 565 | 32.9 | 32.8 | 91 | 94 |
| 56–57 | 74 | 299 | 305 | 973 | 984 | 565 | 535 | 32.8 | 32.6 | 94 | 97 |
| 57–58 | 74 | 305 | 312 | 984 | 991 | 535 | 504 | 32.6 | 32.3 | 97 | 101 |
| 58–59 | 74 | 312 | 297 | 991 | 958 | 504 | 490 | 32.3 | 32.4 | 101 | 98 |
| 59–60 | 78 | 300 | 277 | 975 | 901 | 490 | 403 | 32.4 | 32.0 | 97 | 101 |
| 1960–61 | 117 | 285 | 289 | 941 | 962 | 410 | 385 | 32.2 | 31.8 | 96 | 96 |
| 61–62 | 118 | 289 | 286 | 962 | 958 | 385 | 387 | 31.8 | 31.8 | 96 | 95 |
| 62–63 | 118 | 286 | 287 | 958 | 957 | 387 | 378 | 31.8 | 31.6 | 94 | 94 |
| 63–64 | 118 | 287 | 288 | 957 | 968 | 378 | 373 | 31.6 | 31.4 | 94 | 94 |
| 64–65 | 118 | 288 | 281 | 968 | 960 | 373 | 379 | 31.4 | 31.4 | 94 | 89 |
| 65–66 | 118 | 281 | 276 | 960 | 955 | 379 | 382 | 31.4 | 31.3 | 89 | 85 |
| 66–67 | 118 | 276 | 277 | 955 | 959 | 382 | 374 | 31.3 | 31.1 | 85 | 86 |
| 67–68 | 118 | 277 | 279 | 959 | 967 | 374 | 368 | 31.1 | 30.7 | 86 | 87 |
| 68–69 | 118 | 279 | 283 | 967 | 985 | 368 | 350 | 30.7 | 30.3 | 87 | 88 |
| 69–70 | 119 | 283 | 292 | 987 | 1017 | 350 | 336 | 30.3 | 29.8 | 88 | 94 |
| 1970–71 | 120 | 292 | 289 | 1017 | 1010 | 336 | 326 | 29.8 | 29.8 | 94 | 93 |
| 71–72 | 121 | 290 | 286 | 1013 | 1011 | 326 | 324 | 29.8 | 29.7 | 93 | 90 |
| 72–73 | 121 | 286 | 285 | 1011 | 1012 | 324 | 320 | 29.7 | 29.7 | 90 | 91 |
| 73–74 | 121 | 285 | 291 | 1012 | 1025 | 320 | 304 | 29.7 | 29.5 | 91 | 96 |
| 74–75 | 121 | 291 | 296 | 1025 | 1023 | 304 | 300 | 29.5 | 29.3 | 96 | 102 |
| 75–76 | 121 | 296 | 292 | 1023 | 1018 | 300 | 295 | 29.3 | 29.3 | 102 | 100 |
| 76–77 | 121 | 292 | 288 | 1018 | 990 | 295 | 295 | 29.3 | 29.4 | 100 | 99 |
| 77–78 | 122 | 288 | 282 | 990 | 968 | 295 | 304 | 29.4 | 29.7 | 99 | 98 |
| 78–79 | 122 | 282 | 284 | 968 | 996 | 304 | 302 | 29.7 | 29.5 | 98 | 99 |
| 79–80 | 123 | 284 | 290 | 996 | 1018 | 302 | 305 | 29.5 | 29.4 | 99 | 105 |
| 1980–81 | 124 | 290 | 285 | 1018 | 995 | 305 | 313 | 29.4 | 29.5 | 105 | 105 |
| 81–82 | 124 | 285 | 292 | 995 | 1030 | 313 | 295 | 29.5 | 29.1 | 105 | 108 |
| 82–83 | 124 | 292 | 286 | 1030 | 1010 | 295 | 286 | 29.1 | 29.1 | 108 | 104 |
| 83–84 | 125 | 286 | 273 | 1010 | 969 | 286 | 296 | 29.1 | 29.5 | 104 | 97 |
| 84–85 | 126 | 273 | 269 | 969 | 962 | 296 | 296 | 29.5 | 29.5 | 97 | 96 |
| 85–86 | 132 | 272 | 270 | 970 | 965 | 312 | 301 | 29.6 | 29.7 | 101 | 99 |
| 86–87 | 129 | 269 | 272 | 954 | 972 | 299 | 304 | 29.7 | 29.7 | 102 | 100 |
| 87–88 | 124 | 271 | 270 | 971 | 978 | 303 | 306 | 29.6 | 29.6 | 100 | 99 |
| 88–89 | 120 | 269 | 271 | 974 | 985 | 305 | 305 | 29.6 | 29.6 | 99 | 99 |

and 4. Again, note the stability of the $V$'s in columns 5 and 6; with few exceptions they are between 0.094 and 0.102.

### 4.7. *The Equatorial Grand Canyon in four decades*

The other columns of Table 2-12 are concerned with the canyon model: the minimizing value of $k$, the value of the minimum ($V_k$) and the GDP ratio at the bottom of the canyon ($\bar{R}_k$). The first row of the table shows that the fit of the model is poor in 1950: $V_k = 0.0756$, which is 77 percent of $V = 0.0980$, implying that the model accounts for only 23 percent of the GDP variance. However, the fit improves rapidly over time: $V_k$ becomes smaller than 0.04 after 1960 and in the early 1970s it takes the form $V_k \approx 0.03$ so that the proportion of the GDP variance which is accounted for by the model becomes about 70 percent. Figure 2-4 provides a picture of $V$ and $V_k$ over time (including the discontinuities). The poorer performance of the canyon model in the first half of our sample merits a further investigation; it seems likely that the low income levels (relative to the U.S.) of Western Europe in the immediate postwar period play an important role. We refer to the Appendix for further details.

Columns 9 and 10 show that from 1970 on the minimizing values of $k$ are all between 29 and 30 degrees. The canyon model is a simple one-parameter model, but when it fits (that is, after 1970) it is sufficient to fit this parameter for one year and the fitted value applies to all other years also, at

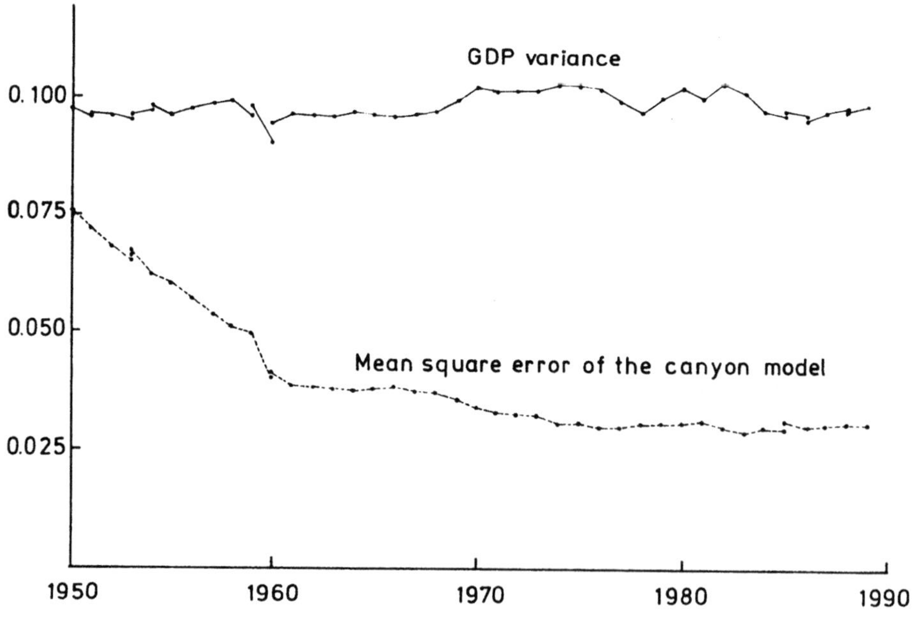


*Figure 2-4.* The GDP variance and the mean square error of the canyon model.

least to a high degree of approximation. The value of $\overline{R}_k$ fluctuates between 0.09 and 0.11 from 1970 on (see columns 11 and 12). Basically, Figure 2-3 applies to all years after 1970. Table 2-12 ends with 1989; time will tell how the model performs in the 1990s.

Note that there is one feature that does change over time: the proportion of the world population living at the bottom of the canyon (the sum of $p_i$ over $i \in C_k$ for the minimizing value of $k$). This proportion is less than 0.55 in the early 1950s; it is just over 0.6 in the early 1970s and it continues to rise (to about two-thirds) in the late 1980s. This result is not surprising, given that the population in the temperate zones declines relative to that in the tropical and subtropical zones (see Table 2-3).

### 4.8. *Conclusions*

Krugman (1991: 95) quoted Robert Solow as saying that efforts to explain differences in national income levels and growth rates usually end in a "blaze of amateur sociology." The present section deals with differences in per capita GDPs, but it does not explain them in terms of concepts from sociology, let alone amateur sociology. Rather, the explanation is in terms of geography and, more specifically, latitude. It cannot claim to be the last word. However, our results do show that more sophisticated approaches (whether based on economics, geography, sociology or any combination) should account for more than 70 percent of the variance of the per capita GDPs.

A comparison with the between-region inequalities in Theil (1989) and in Section 2 is tempting. It is true that the informational inequality measure used in these two places is not entirely comparable to the GDP variance, but there are important similarities: both are population-weighted and the inequality measure has a leading quadratic term when subjected to a Taylor series expansion. Here we find that in 1985 the one-parameter canyon model accounts for 68 percent of the GDP variance of 138 countries. Theil (1989) found for the same year that a five-region classification (which may be viewed as adjusting four parameters) accounts for 76 percent of the inequality among 116 countries, while Table 2-4 in Section 2.2 shows that a seven-region classification (adjusting six parameters) accounts for 88 percent of the inequality among 113 countries. This comparison suggests that latitude may be viewed, statistically speaking, as the principal component of the rich/poor distinction among the countries of the non-communist world.

Again, we emphasize the stability of $k$ in the 1970s and 1980s (columns 9 and 10 of Table 2-12). This stable value is quite close to 30 degrees, which happens to be the horse latitudes discussed in Section 2.1. We should point out that these latitudes are the *trisectors* of the Earth: there are 60 degrees between the North Pole and the 30th parallel North, and also between the 30th parallels North and South, and also between the 30th parallel South and the South Pole. Although these three angles are equal, their populations are far from equal. We mentioned at the end of Section 4.7 that in the 1970s and 1980s the share of the population at the bottom of the canyon is more than 60 percent and rising.[6]

## 5. An analysis of the G-7 countries

In this section we consider the G-7 countries: USA, Canada, Japan, UK, France, Germany (W) and Italy. Note that these seven countries are all in the North.

### 5.1. *Growth and convergence*

Column 2 of Table 2-13 shows that the per capita GDP of the G-7 as a group increased from almost 5200 in 1950 to almost 16000 in 1990. This sharp increase is in contrast to the behavior of the inequality of the seven GDPs. In column 5 we present $J$ (see Section 2.2) for the seven countries, which shows a drastic decline, from 0.183 in 1950 to 0.010 in 1990.

Thus, the G-7 countries became much more affluent on the average, and also much more "equal" (their affluence has "converged" in agreement with Kuznets' hypothesis). How did this happen? To answer this question we group the seven countries into two regions: $R_1$ which is a one-country region consisting of the USA, and $R_2$ which is the Other Six. Columns 3 and 4 of Table 2-13 contain their per capita GDPs, with that of $R_2$ being initially (1950) less than 40 percent of $R_1$ and ultimately (1990) almost 80 percent. Thus, the Other Six succeeded in substantially narrowing the gap between themselves and the USA.

The remainder of Table 2-13 provides an analogous extension of the inequality analysis. Column 6 shows that the regional inequality $J_R$ (USA vs. Other Six) decline drastically. Initially, in 1950, total inequality $J$ was about 0.183 and about 60 percent of this was regional ($J_R/J = 0.596$). Ten years later, in 1960, total inequality was reduced by more than 50 percent, and the regional component of this reduced value was still about 60 percent. Another 10 years later, in 1970, total inequality was reduced even more (by about 70 percent), and the regional component increased to about 80 percent. This 80 percent share continued during the 1970s and 1980s, while total inequality $J$ declined further to about 0.010 in 1990.

Column 8 shows that the inequality $J_2$ among the Other Six declined substantially, from 0.113 in 1950 to less than 0.004 in the mid- and late 1980s; thus, not only have the Other Six converged to the USA on the average,

[6] An intriguing aspect of the horse latitudes is that they (and hence also the edges of the bottom of the canyon) tend to be located in deserts: "on the larger land masses they [the horse latitudes] are regions of deserts, for example, in the northern hemisphere the Sahara, the deserts of the middle east and of central Asia, and those of North America from southeastern California to Texas and northern Mexico. In the southern hemisphere deserts occur in the corresponding belt in Chile, South Africa and Australia" (Benson 1968: 507).

*Table 2-13.* Per capita GDP and inequality of the G-7 countries

| | Per capita GDP | | | Inequality | | | | |
|---|---|---|---|---|---|---|---|---|
| Year (1) | All G-7 (2) | USA (3) | Other six (4) | All G-7 (5) | Regional (6) | Average within region (7) | Among other six (8) | U.S. population share (×100) (9) |
| 1950 | 5169 | 8625 | 3333 | 0.1828 | 0.1090 | 0.0738 | 0.1130 | 34.7 |
| 51 | 5435 | 8987 | 3532 | 0.1709 | 0.1052 | 0.0657 | 0.1009 | 34.9 |
| 52 | 5538 | 8998 | 3670 | 0.1561 | 0.0970 | 0.0591 | 0.0911 | 35.1 |
| 53 | 5734 | 9226 | 3835 | 0.1503 | 0.0930 | 0.0573 | 0.0885 | 35.2 |
| 54 | 5748 | 9006 | 3963 | 0.1363 | 0.0813 | 0.0550 | 0.0852 | 35.4 |
| 55 | 6129 | 9593 | 4218 | 0.1355 | 0.0815 | 0.0539 | 0.0837 | 35.6 |
| 56 | 6256 | 9584 | 4406 | 0.1246 | 0.0729 | 0.0517 | 0.0804 | 35.7 |
| 57 | 6337 | 9530 | 4549 | 0.1136 | 0.0660 | 0.0476 | 0.0742 | 35.9 |
| 58 | 6308 | 9278 | 4633 | 0.1018 | 0.0582 | 0.0435 | 0.0681 | 36.1 |
| 59 | 6619 | 9718 | 4859 | 0.0981 | 0.0580 | 0.0401 | 0.0629 | 36.2 |
| 1960 | 6850 | 9776 | 5177 | 0.0826 | 0.0488 | 0.0338 | 0.0531 | 36.4 |
| 61 | 7061 | 9835 | 5464 | 0.0677 | 0.0417 | 0.0261 | 0.0411 | 36.5 |
| 62 | 7348 | 10234 | 5680 | 0.0656 | 0.0418 | 0.0238 | 0.0375 | 36.6 |
| 63 | 7620 | 10514 | 5939 | 0.0590 | 0.0394 | 0.0196 | 0.0310 | 36.7 |
| 64 | 8008 | 10928 | 6306 | 0.0531 | 0.0365 | 0.0166 | 0.0263 | 36.8 |
| 65 | 8349 | 11492 | 6511 | 0.0560 | 0.0390 | 0.0170 | 0.0269 | 36.9 |
| 66 | 8724 | 11999 | 6804 | 0.0523 | 0.0389 | 0.0134 | 0.0212 | 37.0 |
| 67 | 8967 | 12160 | 7087 | 0.0445 | 0.0352 | 0.0093 | 0.0148 | 37.1 |
| 68 | 9404 | 12555 | 7540 | 0.0379 | 0.0314 | 0.0065 | 0.0104 | 37.2 |
| 69 | 9789 | 12806 | 8008 | 0.0319 | 0.0266 | 0.0054 | 0.0085 | 37.1 |
| 1970 | 10003 | 12725 | 8393 | 0.0254 | 0.0208 | 0.0045 | 0.0072 | 37.2 |
| 71 | 10286 | 13041 | 8651 | 0.0247 | 0.0203 | 0.0045 | 0.0072 | 37.2 |
| 72 | 10767 | 13632 | 9062 | 0.0241 | 0.0201 | 0.0040 | 0.0064 | 37.3 |
| 73 | 11308 | 14226 | 9567 | 0.0224 | 0.0189 | 0.0035 | 0.0055 | 37.4 |
| 74 | 11166 | 13909 | 9529 | 0.0212 | 0.0172 | 0.0040 | 0.0064 | 37.4 |
| 75 | 10920 | 13479 | 9388 | 0.0197 | 0.0157 | 0.0040 | 0.0064 | 37.4 |
| 76 | 11432 | 14087 | 9833 | 0.0198 | 0.0155 | 0.0043 | 0.0069 | 37.6 |
| 77 | 11813 | 14655 | 10093 | 0.0207 | 0.0167 | 0.0040 | 0.0064 | 37.7 |
| 78 | 12273 | 15303 | 10427 | 0.0216 | 0.0178 | 0.0038 | 0.0061 | 37.9 |
| 79 | 12594 | 15408 | 10869 | 0.0183 | 0.0147 | 0.0036 | 0.0058 | 38.0 |
| 1980 | 12588 | 15097 | 11039 | 0.0148 | 0.0118 | 0.0030 | 0.0049 | 38.2 |
| 81 | 12732 | 15339 | 11113 | 0.0156 | 0.0125 | 0.0031 | 0.0050 | 38.3 |
| 82 | 12491 | 14612 | 11166 | 0.0108 | 0.0087 | 0.0021 | 0.0034 | 38.5 |
| 83 | 12778 | 15039 | 11356 | 0.0116 | 0.0095 | 0.0020 | 0.0033 | 38.6 |
| 84 | 13424 | 16154 | 11696 | 0.0150 | 0.0126 | 0.0023 | 0.0038 | 38.8 |
| 85 | 13814 | 16559 | 12066 | 0.0145 | 0.0121 | 0.0024 | 0.0039 | 38.9 |
| 86 | 14139 | 16885 | 12381 | 0.0140 | 0.0117 | 0.0023 | 0.0038 | 39.0 |
| 87 | 14561 | 17332 | 12776 | 0.0135 | 0.0113 | 0.0022 | 0.0037 | 39.2 |
| 88 | 15192 | 17975 | 13388 | 0.0127 | 0.0105 | 0.0022 | 0.0036 | 39.3 |
| 89 | 15609 | 18354 | 13820 | 0.0119 | 0.0098 | 0.0021 | 0.0035 | 39.5 |
| 1990 | 15869 | 18399 | 14220 | 0.0102 | 0.0081 | 0.0021 | 0.0035 | 39.5 |

but the Other Six have also converged toward each other. (The inequality $J_1$ of $R_1$ is obviously zero.) Column 9 will be discussed in Section 5.2.

## 5.2. *Who are the G-7?*

The G-7 countries are frequently referred to as the "seven major industrialized countries." The word industrialized should be interpreted as a contrast to developing or underdeveloped; GDP per capita is one way of measuring the extent to which a country is industrialized in this sense. "Major" means that the country should be sufficiently populous.

Figure 2-5 provides a picture of both variables on a logarithmic scale. Along the horizontal axis we measure GDP per capita of each of the Other Six as a fraction of the U.S. value in the same year. Vertically we measure the population in the same way. We show only the decimal observations 1950, 1960, . . . , 1990 in order not to overburden the picture.

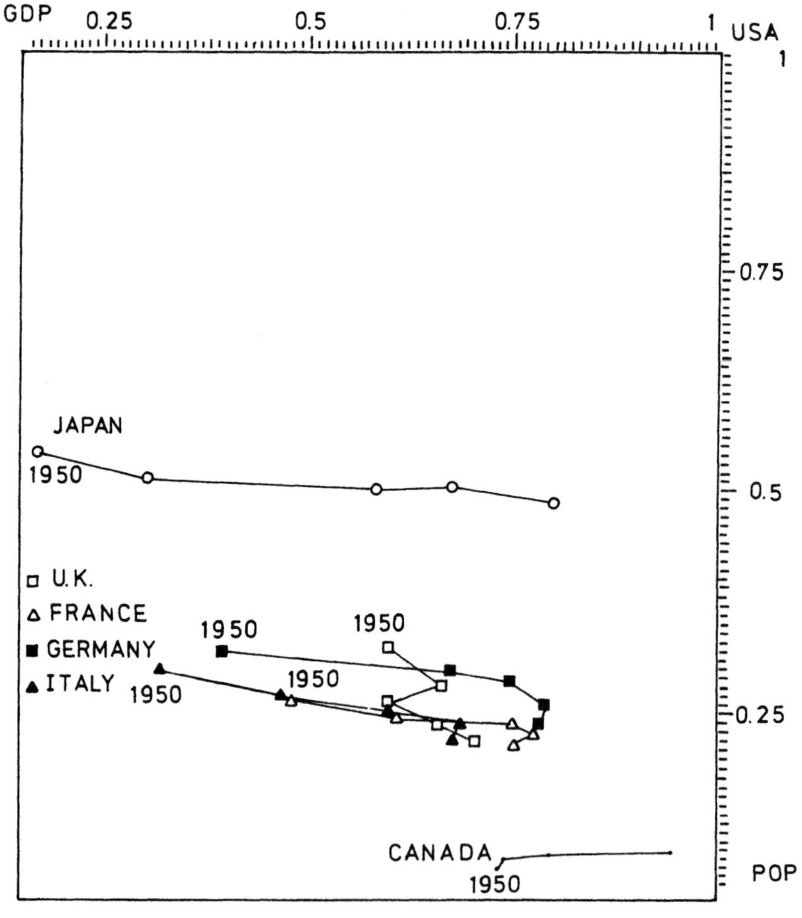


*Figure 2-5.* USA vs. Other Six G-7 countries, 1950–1990.

The figure confirms the general decline of income inequality by a general movement from left to right for each of the six countries. The most dramatic of these movements is the case of Japan whose GDP per capita increased from 17 percent of the U.S. value in 1950 to more than 80 percent in 1990. At the same time, the figure indicates that while the Japanese economy has been approaching the U.S. economy in terms of GDP per capita, the size of the Japanese economy has declined from a population perspective. The population shares of five G-7 countries outside North America have all declined. Canada and USA are immigration countries; their population shares in the G-7 went up. Column 9 of Table 2-12 shows this for the USA.

Note that the G-7 is *not* a club of the richest countries. Norway, Switzerland and Australia all have per capita GDPs exceeding that of Italy in 1990 (Italy is the least affluent of the G-7), but these three countries have populations well below that of Canada (which has the smallest population among the G-7). The G-7 is the club of the most populous countries among those which satisfy a minimum standard of affluence.

## APPENDIX

### More on the Equatorial Grand Canyon

The use of binary countries maximizes the use of the available data in two respects: it exploits the largest number of years (four decades in this case) and it uses the maximum number of countries for each pair of successive years. The disadvantage of this procedure is that it leads to discontinuities (see Fig. 2-4); its variables take two values in each year, $t$ being represented in both $(t-1, t)$ and $(t, t+1)$.

We can avoid this disadvantage by confining ourselves to a subperiod of the four decades and a subset of the 138 countries so that each country in the subset is represented in the entire period. For this purpose we return to Section 2.1 with its 113 countries in 1961–1986; as in Section 4, we delete two city-states so that 111 countries remain. Of course, when doing so we lose a lot of data, but this alternative procedure has the additional advantage of verifying the sensitivity of the canyon model to deleting certain observations.

The results are summarized in Table 2-14, which should be compared with Table 2-12. Column 2 of Table 2-14 gives world per capita GDP, measured as a fraction of the U.S. value in the same year. These numbers are all very close to the corresponding values in columns 3 and 4 of Table 2-12. The same holds for the GDP variance in column 3 of Table 2-14 when compared with columns 5 and 6 of Table 2-12, and also for the minimum mean square error in column 4 of Table 2-14 (compared with columns 7 and 8 of Table 2-12). The minimizing $k$ for the 111 countries is shown in the last column of Table 2-14. These $k$ values gradually decline from almost 32 degrees in the early 1960s to values between 29 and 30 degrees in the 1970s and 1980s. This behavior of $k$ is also close to that in Table 2-12 (columns 7 and 8).

We shall find it convenient to fix the bottom of the canyon at $C_{30}$ = (–30, 30). This will enable us to trace the performance of the canyon model over time with a fixed value $k = 30$ (rather than a $k$ which changes from year to year). A comparison of columns 4 and 5 of Table 2-14 shows that this fixed value raises the mean square error only slightly. Also, columns 6 and 7 indicate that the GDP per capita at the bottom of the canyon is virtually unaffected. Its value is about 10 percent of the U.S. value in the same year, as it is in columns 11 and 12 of Table 2-12.

We proceed to analyze the performance of the canyon model in its four zones, starting in the South and then moving in Northern direction: $Z_1 = S_{30}$ (the South Slope), $Z_2 = C_{30}$ (the bottom of the canyon), $Z_3 = N_{30}$ (the North Slope), and $Z_4 = F$ (the Northern Plateau). We define $P_g$ as the population share of $Z_g$ and $M_g$ as its arithmetic mean error:

$$P_g = \sum_{i \in Z_g} p_i, \qquad M_g = \sum_{i \in Z_g} (p_i/P_g)(R_i - \hat{R}_i)$$

*Table 2-14.* The Canyon model for 111 countries

| Year (1) | $\bar{R}$ (2) | $V$ (3) | $V_k$ (4) | $V_{30}$ (5) | $\bar{R}_k$ (6) | $\bar{R}_{30}$ (7) | $k$ (8) |
|---|---|---|---|---|---|---|---|
| 1961 | 0.289 | 0.0963 | 0.0385 | 0.0394 | 0.096 | 0.096 | 31.8 |
| 62 | 0.286 | 0.0959 | 0.0387 | 0.0396 | 0.094 | 0.094 | 31.8 |
| 63 | 0.287 | 0.0959 | 0.0378 | 0.0386 | 0.094 | 0.095 | 31.6 |
| 64 | 0.288 | 0.0969 | 0.0373 | 0.0379 | 0.094 | 0.094 | 31.4 |
| 65 | 0.281 | 0.0961 | 0.0379 | 0.0385 | 0.089 | 0.089 | 31.4 |
| 66 | 0.276 | 0.0957 | 0.0382 | 0.0387 | 0.085 | 0.085 | 31.3 |
| 67 | 0.277 | 0.0960 | 0.0374 | 0.0377 | 0.086 | 0.086 | 31.1 |
| 68 | 0.279 | 0.0969 | 0.0368 | 0.0369 | 0.086 | 0.087 | 30.7 |
| 69 | 0.284 | 0.0989 | 0.0351 | 0.0351 | 0.088 | 0.088 | 30.3 |
| 1970 | 0.293 | 0.1020 | 0.0338 | 0.0338 | 0.094 | 0.094 | 29.8 |
| 71 | 0.292 | 0.1019 | 0.0329 | 0.0329 | 0.093 | 0.093 | 29.8 |
| 72 | 0.288 | 0.1017 | 0.0327 | 0.0327 | 0.091 | 0.091 | 29.7 |
| 73 | 0.287 | 0.1018 | 0.0323 | 0.0323 | 0.091 | 0.091 | 29.7 |
| 74 | 0.293 | 0.1030 | 0.0307 | 0.0307 | 0.096 | 0.096 | 29.5 |
| 75 | 0.298 | 0.1029 | 0.0303 | 0.0304 | 0.102 | 0.102 | 29.3 |
| 76 | 0.295 | 0.1025 | 0.0298 | 0.0299 | 0.100 | 0.100 | 29.3 |
| 77 | 0.290 | 0.0996 | 0.0298 | 0.0299 | 0.100 | 0.100 | 29.4 |
| 78 | 0.284 | 0.0974 | 0.0306 | 0.0307 | 0.099 | 0.099 | 29.7 |
| 79 | 0.286 | 0.1002 | 0.0304 | 0.0305 | 0.099 | 0.099 | 29.5 |
| 1980 | 0.292 | 0.1024 | 0.0308 | 0.0309 | 0.105 | 0.105 | 29.4 |
| 81 | 0.287 | 0.1002 | 0.0316 | 0.0317 | 0.105 | 0.105 | 29.5 |
| 82 | 0.294 | 0.1037 | 0.0298 | 0.0300 | 0.109 | 0.109 | 29.1 |
| 83 | 0.288 | 0.1016 | 0.0289 | 0.0291 | 0.104 | 0.104 | 29.1 |
| 84 | 0.275 | 0.0976 | 0.0299 | 0.0299 | 0.097 | 0.097 | 29.5 |
| 85 | 0.273 | 0.0974 | 0.0301 | 0.0302 | 0.097 | 0.097 | 29.5 |
| 86 | 0.271 | 0.0972 | 0.0294 | 0.0294 | 0.096 | 0.096 | 29.6 |

A positive (negative) $M_g$ indicates that the observed per capita GDPs of $Z_g$ are on average larger (smaller) than the model predicts. We have $M_2 = 0$ because for $i \in Z_2$ we define $\hat{R}_i$ as the region's per capita GDP ($\bar{R}_k = \bar{R}_{30}$).

Columns 2 to 5 of Table 2-15 contain the population shares of the four zones. The share of $Z_2 = C_{30}$ increases uninterruptedly at the expense of the three other zones. The share of the South Slope is only about 2 percent; it is smaller than shown in Table 2-3 (column 4) because South Africa's most populous city (Johannesburg) is inside $C_{30}$.

Columns 6 to 8 contain the $M_g$'s (except $M_2 = 0$). The mean $M_1$ of $Z_1 = S_{30}$ is consistently positive, but it is much smaller in the mid-1980s than in the first 15 years. For $Z_3 = N_{30}$ the mean changes from negative to positive in the early 1970s; this mean is closer to zero than the others (except $M_2 = 0$) in all years. By far the largest mean is that of $Z_4 = F$, consisting mostly of countries in North-West Europe. Also, this mean is consistently negative. This results from the model's prediction that the per capita GDPs of these

*Table 2-15.* The four zones of the Canyon model

| | 1,000 $P_g$ | | | | 1,000 $M_g$ | | | 10,000 $W_g$ | | | |
|---|---|---|---|---|---|---|---|---|---|---|---|
| Year (1) | $Z_1$ (2) | $Z_2$ (3) | $Z_3$ (4) | $Z_4$ (5) | $Z_1$ (6) | $Z_3$ (7) | $Z_4$ (8) | $Z_1$ (9) | $Z_2$ (10) | $Z_3$ (11) | $Z_4$ (12) |
| 1961 | 23 | 595 | 265 | 117 | 121 | −67 | −321 | 513 | 55 | 833 | 1104 |
| 62 | 22 | 598 | 264 | 116 | 107 | −64 | −328 | 536 | 55 | 828 | 1149 |
| 63 | 22 | 601 | 262 | 115 | 99 | −57 | −327 | 583 | 55 | 796 | 1138 |
| 64 | 22 | 603 | 261 | 114 | 108 | −52 | −316 | 612 | 58 | 802 | 1063 |
| 65 | 22 | 606 | 260 | 112 | 100 | −54 | −327 | 524 | 56 | 815 | 1134 |
| 66 | 22 | 608 | 258 | 111 | 94 | −49 | −339 | 520 | 55 | 802 | 1214 |
| 67 | 22 | 611 | 257 | 110 | 91 | −40 | −336 | 527 | 56 | 781 | 1187 |
| 68 | 22 | 615 | 255 | 108 | 95 | −30 | −330 | 603 | 57 | 771 | 1146 |
| 69 | 22 | 617 | 254 | 107 | 104 | −20 | −310 | 622 | 58 | 756 | 1027 |
| 1970 | 22 | 620 | 253 | 105 | 118 | −5 | −284 | 699 | 64 | 743 | 896 |
| 71 | 22 | 623 | 251 | 104 | 120 | −6 | −276 | 682 | 65 | 741 | 842 |
| 72 | 22 | 626 | 250 | 103 | 107 | −3 | −278 | 645 | 64 | 748 | 836 |
| 73 | 22 | 629 | 248 | 101 | 97 | 1 | −276 | 635 | 65 | 746 | 821 |
| 74 | 22 | 631 | 247 | 100 | 109 | 7 | −256 | 655 | 76 | 695 | 731 |
| 75 | 21 | 634 | 246 | 98 | 107 | 13 | −245 | 731 | 83 | 690 | 673 |
| 76 | 21 | 638 | 245 | 96 | 88 | 15 | −245 | 689 | 84 | 677 | 675 |
| 77 | 21 | 641 | 244 | 95 | 76 | 12 | −259 | 576 | 79 | 680 | 739 |
| 78 | 21 | 644 | 242 | 93 | 64 | 3 | −271 | 586 | 77 | 702 | 797 |
| 79 | 21 | 646 | 241 | 91 | 76 | 9 | −250 | 564 | 85 | 724 | 692 |
| 1980 | 21 | 649 | 240 | 90 | 91 | 12 | −231 | 630 | 95 | 745 | 612 |
| 81 | 21 | 652 | 239 | 89 | 82 | 8 | −246 | 648 | 93 | 758 | 697 |
| 82 | 21 | 655 | 238 | 87 | 66 | 23 | −210 | 663 | 92 | 762 | 514 |
| 83 | 21 | 658 | 236 | 86 | 66 | 22 | −219 | 730 | 76 | 760 | 545 |
| 84 | 20 | 660 | 235 | 84 | 54 | 11 | −252 | 683 | 68 | 768 | 710 |
| 85 | 20 | 663 | 234 | 83 | 51 | 11 | −253 | 705 | 67 | 785 | 718 |
| 86 | 20 | 666 | 233 | 81 | 43 | 9 | −247 | 669 | 65 | 779 | 692 |

countries are equal to that of the USA. Such a prediction is too optimistic, although the mean error becomes a bit smaller after the mid-1970s.

The last four columns of Table 2-15 deal with the mean square errors of the canyon model in each zone:

$$W_g = \sum_{i \in Z_g} (p_i/P_g)(R_i - \hat{R}_i)^2$$

Note that these $W_g$'s satisfy $\sum_g P_g W_g = V_{30}$. Also note that during the 1960s $W_4$ exceeds the other $W_g$'s substantially, but that $W_1$, $W_3$ and $W_4$ are of comparable size after the mid-1970s. For the central zone, $Z_2 = C_{30}$, $W_2$ is much smaller but this does not mean a larger relative accuracy, since the per capita GDPs of $Z_2$ are mostly quite low.

## References


Ahluwalia, M.S. (1976). "Income distribution and development: Some stylized facts." *American Economic Review* 66: 128–135.

Benson, L. (1968). "Wild flower." *Encyclopedia Brittanica* 23: 506–509.

Geary, R.C. (1958). "A note on the comparison of exchange rates and purchasing power between countries." *Journal of the Royal Statistical Society*, Series A, 121: 97–99.

Khamis, S.H. (1967). "Some problems relating to the international comparability and fluctuations of production volume indicators." *Bulletin of the International Statistical Institute* 42, Part 1: 213–230.

Khamis, S.H. (1970). "Properties and conditions for the existence of a new type of index numbers." *Sankhyā* Series B, 32: 81–98.

Khamis, S.H. (1972). "A new system of index numbers for national and international purposes." *Journal of the Royal Statistical Society*, Series A, 135: 96–121.

Kravis, I.B., Heston, A.W. and Summers, R. (1978a). *International Comparisons of Real Product and Purchasing Power*. Baltimore, Md.: The Johns Hopkins University Press.

Kravis, I.B., Heston, A.W. and Summers, R. (1978b). "Real GDP per capita for more than one hundred countries." *Economic Journal* 88: 215–242.

Kravis, I.B., Heston, A.W. and Summers, R. (1982). *World Product and Income: International Comparisons of Real Gross Product*. Baltimore, Md.: The Johns Hopkins University Press.

Kravis, I.B., Kenessey, Z., Heston, A.W. and Summers, R. (1975). *A System of International Comparisons of Gross Product and Purchasing Power*. Baltimore, Md.: The Johns Hopkins University Press.

Krugman, P. (1991). *Geography and Trade*. Cambridge, Mass.: MIT Press.

Kuznets, S. (1955). "Economic growth and income inequality." *American Economic Review* 45: 1–28.

Papanek, G.F. and Kyn, O. (1986). "The effect on income distribution of development, the growth rate and economic strategy." *Journal of Development Economics* 23: 55–65.

Paukert, F. (1973). "Income distribution at different levels of development: A survey of the evidence." *International Labour Review* 108: 97–125.

Raj, B. and Koerts, J. (1992). *Henri Theil's Contributions to Economics and Econometrics*. Three volumes. Dordrecht/Boston/London: Kluwer Academic Publishers.

Ram, R. (1989). "Level of development and income inequality: An extension of the Kuznets hypothesis to the world economy." *Kyklos* 42: 73–88.

Sanders, F. (1991). "Zone, climatic." *The Encyclopedia Americana* (International Edition), Vol. 29: pp. 793–794. Danbury, Connecticut.

Summers, R. and Heston, A.W. (1984). "Improved international comparisons of real product and its composition, 1950–80." *Review of Income and Wealth* 30: 207–262.

Summers, R. and Heston, A.W. (1988). "A new set of international comparisons of real product and price levels: Estimates for 130 countries, 1950–1985." *Review of Income and Wealth* 34: 1–25.

Summers, R. and Heston, A.W. (1991). "The Penn World Table (Mark 5): An expanded set of international comparisons, 1950–1988." *Quarterly Journal of Economics* 106: 327–368.

Summers, R. and Heston, A.W. (1993). Supplement to Summers and Heston (1991) in the form of a diskette with data through 1990.

Theil, H. (1979). "World income inequality and its components." *Economics Letters* 2: 99–102. Also in Raj and Koerts (1992), Ch. 52.

Theil, H. (1989). "The development of international inequality, 1960–1985." *Journal of Econometrics* 42: 145–155. Also in Raj and Koerts (1992), Ch. 53.

Theil, H. and Chen, D. (1995). "The Equatorial Grand Canyon (Dedicated to the memory of Pieter Hennipman)." *De Economist* 143: 317–327.

Theil, H. and Deepak, S.D. (1994). "The GDPs of seven major regions, 1950–1990." *Empirical Economics* 19: 517–522.

Theil, H. and Finke, R. (1983). "The distance from the equator as an instrumental variable." *Economics Letters* 13: 357–360.

Theil, H. and Galvez, J. (1995). "On latitude and affluence: The Equatorial Grand Canyon." *Empirical Economics* 20: 163–166.

Theil, H. and Seale, J.L., Jr. (1994). "The geographic distribution of world income, 1950–1990 (Dedicated to the memory of Jan Tinbergen)." *De Economist* 142: 387–419.

CHAPTER 3

# The spatial autocorrelation of per capita GDPs

HENRI THEIL, CHARLES B. MOSS and DONGLING CHEN

**Abstract.** This paper develops a population-weighted measure of spatial autocorrelation. It is applied to PPP-based data on GDPs for six regions (PPP = purchasing power parity).

The availability of per capita GDPs of different countries in real terms, all expressed in the same unit, enables the analyst to apply certain concepts from quantitative geography. One such concept is spatial autocorrelation, which goes back to the (unweighted) proposals made by the statisticians R.C. Geary and P.A.P. Moran in the 1950s,[1] but for our purpose it is more attractive to use a measure which is population-weighted. More specifically, consider a contiguous region consisting of $n$ countries. We write $x_i$ for the per capita GDP and $p_i$ for the population share of country $i$; then

$$\bar{x} = \sum_{i=1}^{n} p_i x_i \quad \text{and} \quad V = \sum_{i=1}^{n} p_i (x_i - \bar{x})^2$$

are, respectively, the per capita GDP of the region and the variance of the per capita GDPs of the separate countries.[2] The variance is population-weighted.

It is readily verified that

$$\sum_{i=1}^{n} \sum_{j=1}^{n} p_i p_j (x_i - x_j)^2 = 2V$$

We shall use this result to define a measure of spatial correlation. Let $\Pi_B$ be the set of pairs of countries $(i, j)$ that share a border of positive length. The weighted *sum of squares* of the per capita GDP differences of countries that share such a border is now defined as

$$\Sigma_B p_i p_j (x_i - x_j)^2$$

[1] For a more recent survey see Odland (1988).

[2] This variance plays a prominent role in the Equatorial Grand Canyon model developed by Theil and Galvez (1995), Theil and Chen (1995), and Chapter 2 of this volume.

where $\Sigma_B$ stands for summation over all pairs $(i, j)$ that fall under $\Pi_B$. The corresponding *mean square* (the mean square border difference) is

$$\text{MSBD} = (1/\theta_B)\ \Sigma_B p_i p_j (x_i - x_j)^2 \quad \text{where} \quad \theta_B = \Sigma_B p_i p_j$$

Similarly, write $\Pi_N$ for the set of country pairs $(i, j)$ that share no border of positive length. The mean square non-border difference is

$$\text{MSND} = (1/\theta_N)\ \Sigma_N p_i p_j (x_i - x_j)^2 \quad \text{where} \quad \theta_N = \Sigma_N p_i p_j$$

with $\Sigma_N$ defined as the summation over all country pairs $(i, j)$ that fall under $\Pi_N$. Note that the total number of elements of the combined sets $(\Pi_B, \Pi_N)$ is $n(n - 1)$.

Our measure of spatial correlation is the ratio MSBD/MSND. This ratio is 1 when there is no such correlation, but intuition suggests that the ratio is normally less than 1. Also note the unit-sum rule,

$$\theta_B + \theta_N + H = 1 \quad \text{where} \quad H = \sum_{i=1}^{n} p_i^2$$

with $H$ defined as the Hirschman-Herfindahl concentration index (in this case: the concentration of the population across countries). Note further that $\theta_B(\text{MSBD}) + \theta_N(\text{MSND}) = 2V$.

We proceed to apply these results to six regions. One of these is the Americas, represented by 20 countries (see the upper part of Table 3-1) located on the continent of the Western Hemisphere. The second region is Africa, represented by 42 countries located on that continent (see Table 3-1). The third region is Little Europe, consisting of 14 countries (see Table 3-1); note that we regard Denmark and Sweden as sharing a border in spite of their separation by the Sound. For Greater Europe we act as if France and UK share a border, and similarly for Greece and Italy. Greater Europe consists of 18 countries, viz., the 14 of Little Europe plus Greece, Ireland, Turkey and UK. Little South Asia consists of the 11 countries listed at the bottom of Table 3-1. Greater South Asia enlarges this region by adding Greece and Turkey on the West, Sri Lanka on the South, and Malaysia, Singapore, Indonesia, Papua New Guinea and the Philippines on the East. India and Sri Lanka are regarded as sharing a border; Indonesia is regarded as sharing borders with Singapore, Malaysia, the Philippines and Papua New Guinea.

Figure 3-1 illustrates the unit-sum rule on $\theta_B$, $\theta_N$ and $H$ by means of a triangular array. These three fractions depend only on the population shares of the countries involved. Since these shares change slowly over time, we confine ourselves to one year (1985) in Fig. 3-1.

However, there is considerable variation across regions. The dominance of India in Little South Asia is reflected by the "high" position (near point $H$) of this region in the triangular display. The other extreme is Africa; this continent is represented by as many as 42 countries, none of which dominates the others in terms of population. Also, and not surprisingly, the large number of countries pushes Africa's position away from the left side of the

*Table 3-1.* Eighty-seven countries in four regions

| | | |
|---|---|---|
| | *20 countries in the Americas* | |
| Argentina | Ecuador | Panama |
| Bolivia | El Salvador | Paraguay |
| Brazil | Guatemala | Peru |
| Canada | Guyana | Uruguay |
| Chile | Honduras | USA |
| Colombia | Mexico | Venezuela |
| Costa Rica | Nicaragua | |
| | *42 countries in Africa* | |
| Algeria | Ghana | Nigeria |
| Angola | Guinea | Rwanda |
| Benin | Guinea-Bissau | Senegal |
| Botswana | Ivory Coast | Sierra Leone |
| Burkina Faso | Kenya | Somalia |
| Burundi | Lesotho | South Africa |
| Cameroon | Liberia | Swaziland |
| Central African R. | Malawi | Tanzania |
| Chad | Mali | Togo |
| Congo | Mauritania | Tunisia |
| Egypt | Morocco | Uganda |
| Ethiopia | Mozambique | Zaire |
| Gabon | Namibia | Zambia |
| Gambia | Niger | Zimbabwe |
| | *14 countries in Little Europe* | |
| Austria | Germany (W) | Portugal |
| Belgium | Italy | Spain |
| Denmark | Luxembourg | Sweden |
| Finland | Netherlands | Switzerland |
| France | Norway | |
| | *11 countries in Little South Asia* | |
| Bangladesh | Israel | Pakistan |
| India | Jordan | Syria |
| Iran | Myanmar | Thailand |
| Iraq | Nepal | |

triangular base (point $\theta_B$, representing bordering countries) toward the right side ($\theta_N$, representing more distant countries).

The ratios MSBD/MSND in Table 3-2 are all less than 1;[3] this is as we could intuitively expect, rich countries having usually rich neighbors and poor countries having usually poor neighbors. Columns 2 and 3 show that in the

[3] These ratios have been computed from GDPs expressed in 1985 international prices; see Summers and Heston (1993).

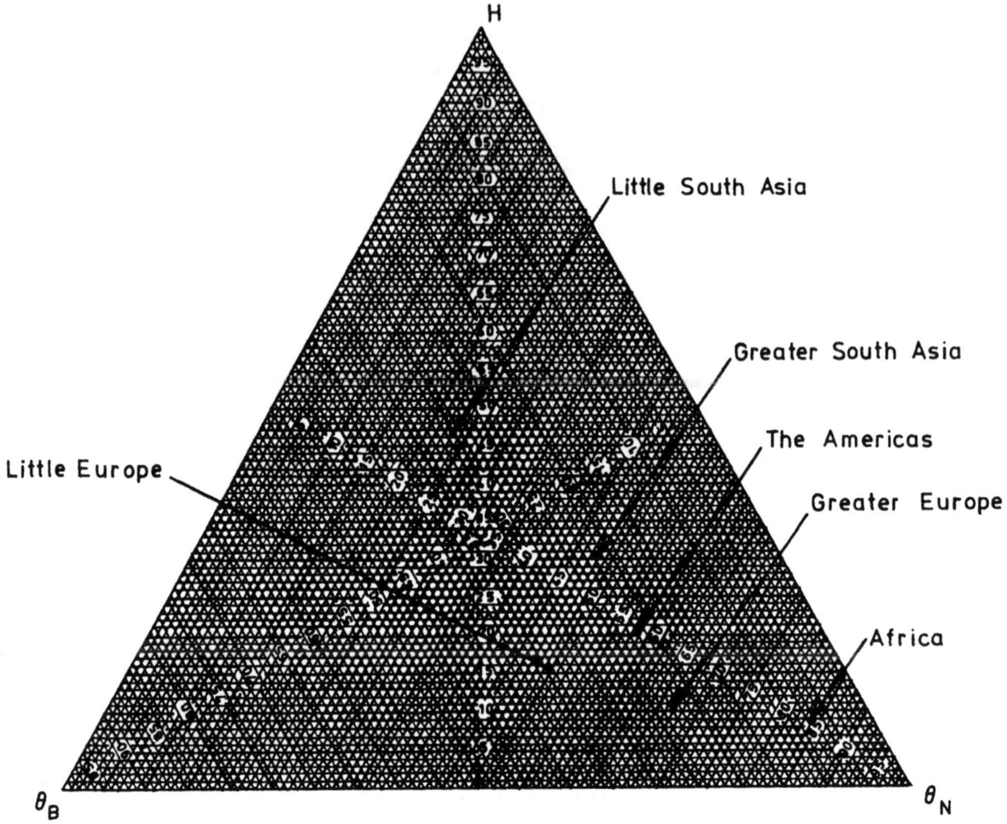


*Figure 3-1.* Triangular array for $\theta_B$, $\theta_N$ and $H$.

Americas and in Africa, the mean square border difference is about one-half of the mean square non-border difference. The ratios of these two continents do not show any clear trend, neither upward nor downward. This is different from the behavior of these ratios in Western Europe. The ratios of Little Europe decline from more than 0.7 in the early 1950s to less than 0.4 in the late 1980s, while those of Greater Europe decline from more than 0.4 to less than 0.15. Such a decline means that differences between neighbors tend to decrease relative to the differences between more distant countries. The ratios of South Asia are quite small, particularly those of Little South Asia. This reflects the fact that this region's most populous country (India) is surrounded by countries with similarly low per capita GDPs.

*Table 3-2.* The ratios MSBD/MSND of six regions[a]

| Year (1) | The Americas (2) | Africa (3) | Little Europe (4) | Greater Europe (5) | Little S. Asia (6) | Greater S. Asia (7) |
|---|---|---|---|---|---|---|
| 1950 | 0.571 | . | 0.777 | 0.444 | . | . |
| 51 | 0.566 | . | 0.834 | 0.453 | . | . |
| 52 | 0.559 | . | 0.720 | 0.412 | . | . |
| 53 | 0.581 | . | 0.633 | 0.393 | . | . |
| 54 | 0.578 | . | 0.599 | 0.362 | . | . |
| 55 | 0.578 | . | 0.538 | 0.345 | . | . |
| 56 | 0.556 | . | 0.581 | 0.354 | . | . |
| 57 | 0.557 | . | 0.580 | 0.365 | . | . |
| 58 | 0.551 | . | 0.524 | 0.335 | . | . |
| 59 | 0.565 | . | 0.500 | 0.329 | . | . |
| 1960 | 0.562 | . | 0.489 | 0.312 | 0.050 | 0.165 |
| 61 | 0.575 | . | 0.513 | 0.309 | 0.046 | 0.147 |
| 62 | 0.578 | . | 0.516 | 0.300 | 0.041 | 0.149 |
| 63 | 0.559 | . | 0.526 | 0.295 | 0.048 | 0.148 |
| 64 | 0.547 | . | 0.517 | 0.290 | 0.043 | 0.134 |
| 65 | 0.547 | 0.477 | 0.513 | 0.281 | 0.047 | 0.148 |
| 66 | 0.543 | 0.475 | 0.533 | 0.285 | 0.048 | 0.142 |
| 67 | 0.538 | 0.465 | 0.564 | 0.284 | 0.056 | 0.154 |
| 68 | 0.534 | 0.464 | 0.530 | 0.263 | 0.050 | 0.142 |
| 69 | 0.534 | 0.453 | 0.524 | 0.265 | 0.049 | 0.139 |
| 1970 | 0.533 | 0.452 | 0.555 | 0.300 | 0.046 | 0.136 |
| 71 | 0.544 | 0.445 | 0.636 | 0.307 | 0.040 | 0.119 |
| 72 | 0.543 | 0.450 | 0.645 | 0.280 | 0.041 | 0.117 |
| 73 | 0.544 | 0.445 | 0.630 | 0.247 | 0.046 | 0.133 |
| 74 | 0.533 | 0.463 | 0.656 | 0.252 | 0.044 | 0.128 |
| 75 | 0.508 | 0.485 | 0.542 | 0.229 | 0.043 | 0.119 |
| 76 | 0.526 | 0.476 | 0.462 | 0.212 | 0.045 | 0.126 |
| 77 | 0.555 | 0.504 | 0.460 | 0.208 | 0.045 | 0.128 |
| 78 | 0.536 | 0.510 | 0.442 | 0.199 | 0.041 | 0.118 |
| 79 | 0.505 | 0.484 | 0.408 | 0.191 | 0.033 | 0.115 |
| 1980 | 0.466 | 0.490 | 0.395 | 0.191 | 0.032 | 0.119 |
| 81 | 0.417 | 0.506 | 0.424 | 0.203 | 0.033 | 0.114 |
| 82 | 0.441 | 0.492 | 0.465 | 0.210 | 0.036 | 0.125 |
| 83 | 0.483 | 0.478 | 0.420 | 0.188 | 0.036 | 0.126 |
| 84 | 0.491 | 0.478 | 0.367 | 0.177 | 0.039 | 0.129 |
| 85 | 0.488 | 0.465 | 0.361 | 0.172 | 0.043 | 0.130 |
| 86 | 0.531 | 0.466 | 0.369 | 0.173 | 0.044 | 0.122 |
| 87 | 0.540 | . | 0.369 | 0.160 | . | . |
| 88 | . | . | 0.371 | 0.148 | . | . |
| 89 | . | . | 0.377 | 0.140 | . | . |
| 1990 | . | . | 0.368 | 0.139 | . | . |

[a] Dots indicate that data are missing for one or several countries of the region.

## References

Odland, J. (1988). *Spatial Autocorrelation*. Newbury Park, Calif.: Sage Publications.
Summers, R. and Heston, A.W. (1991). "The Penn World Table (Mark 5): An expanded set of international comparisons, 1950–1988." *Quarterly Journal of Economics* 106: 327–368.
Summers, R. and Heston, A.W. (1993). Supplement to Summers and Heston (1991) in the form of a diskette with data through 1990.
Theil, H. and Galvez, J. (1995). "On latitude and affluence: The Equatorial and Grand Canyon." *Empirical Economics* 20: 163–166.
Theil, H. and Chen, D. (1995). "The Equatorial Grand Canyon (Dedicated to the memory of Pieter Hennipman)." *De Economist* 143: 317–327.

CHAPTER 4

# The informational fit and fitting of cross-country demand systems

HENRI THEIL and DONGLING CHEN

**Abstract.** Measures from statistical information theory are applied to cross-country demand analysis for several purposes. One is to measure the fit of a model for each country separately, including the Strobel decomposition of this fit. A second purpose is to use this measure of fit for statistically estimating the model. It is shown that this method is superior to maximum likelihood when the sample is small but the model is not. A third purpose is to search for outliers. It is argued that a major source of outliers is the underreported food consumption in a number of less developed countries.

## 1. A lemma and an informational measure of fit

Our starting point is a simple lemma. It states that for any positive number $x$,

$$\begin{aligned} \log_e x &= x - 1 \quad \text{if} \quad x = 1 \\ &< x - 1 \quad \text{if} \quad x \neq 1 \end{aligned} \tag{1.1}$$

*Proof:* Draw the curve $y = \log_e x$ and the straight line $z = x - 1$. The two intersect at $x = 1$. The slope of the curve is $dy/dx = 1/x$, which is larger than 1 (the slope of the straight line) for $x < 1$, and smaller than 1 for $x > 1$. Therefore, the curve is below the straight line everywhere except at $x = 1$. It should be understood from now on that all logs in this chapter are natural logs.

We proceed to apply the lemma to predicted and observed budget shares. For each of $n$ consumer goods, let $w_{ic}$ be the observed per capita budget share of good $i$ in country $c$. Let there be a model which predicts that this budget share is $\hat{w}_{ic}$; both $w_{ic}$ and $\hat{w}_{ic}$ are positive and add up to 1 when summed over $i = 1, \ldots, n$. We apply (1.1) to $x = \hat{w}_{ic}/w_{ic}$:

$$\begin{aligned} \log(\hat{w}_{ic}/w_{ic}) &= (\hat{w}_{ic} - w_{ic})/w_{ic} \quad \text{if} \quad \hat{w}_{ic} = w_{ic} \\ &< (\hat{w}_{ic} - w_{ic})/w_{ic} \quad \text{if} \quad \hat{w}_{ic} \neq w_{ic} \end{aligned}$$

We multiply both sides by $w_{ic}$ and find, after minor rearrangements, that

$$I_{ic} = \hat{w}_{ic} - w_{ic} + w_{ic} \log(w_{ic}/\hat{w}_{ic}) \tag{1.2}$$

is always positive except when the prediction is perfect ($\hat{w}_{ic} = w_{ic}$, in which case $I_{ic} = 0$). The result (1.2) is from Strobel (1982).

Table 4-1 illustrates the $I_{ic}$'s for 15 countries (listed in the last column) and for the following 10 broad consumption groups:

1. Food
2. Beverages and tobacco
3. Clothing and footwear
4. Gross rent and fuel
5. House furnishings and operations
6. Medical care
7. Transport and communications
8. Recreation
9. Education
10. Other consumption expenditures

The names of these groups are also shown (in abbreviated form) in the top row of Table 4-1.

We need one further development before discussing the numbers of the table. Summation of both sides of (1.2) over $i$ yields

$$I_c = \sum_{i=1}^{n} I_{ic} \tag{1.3}$$

where

$$I_c = \sum_{i=1}^{n} w_{ic} \log(w_{ic}/\hat{w}_{ic}) \tag{1.4}$$

Whereas $I_{ic}$ is a measure of the "badness" of fit for $\hat{w}_{ic}$ with respect to $w_{ic}$, $I_c$ measures the fit of all predictions $\hat{w}_{ic}, \ldots, \hat{w}_{nc}$ with respect to all observed budget shares $w_{1c}, \ldots, w_{nc}$. In the language of statistical information theory (see Appendix A) we can view the right side (1.4) as the expected information of the message which transforms the predicted budget shares as "prior probabilities" into the observed shares as "posterior probabilities." Obviously, the larger this information, the worse the predictions are; hence, $I_c$ is known as the information inaccuracy of the predictions and the $I_{ic}$'s as the Strobel components of this inaccuracy. The major justification of this definition is the *additivity* of the information concept. Appendix A provides further details.

We return to Table 4-1 and note that the predicted budget shares have been obtained from a cross-country demand model about which we shall have a great deal to say in Section 5. The figures in the table refer to the year 1970. The $I_{ic}$'s are shown in the first 10 columns and the $I_c$'s in column 11. The arithmetic mean of the 15 entries in each column is shown in the last row of the table; this mean is an obvious summary measure, given the additivity of the information concept. The entries in column 11 for France, Italy and the USA are all much smaller than the arithmetic mean, thus indi-

*Table 4-1.* Information inaccuracies and their Strobel components

| Food (1) | Beverages (2) | Clothing (3) | Rent (4) | House (5) | Medical (6) | Transport (7) | Recreation (8) | Education (9) | Other (10) | Sum (11) | Country (12) |
|---|---|---|---|---|---|---|---|---|---|---|---|
| 4 | 9 | 0 | 3 | 46 | 16 | 11 | 25 | 17 | 16 | 147 | Belgium |
| 67 | 13 | 3 | 33 | 6 | 13 | 52 | 2 | 9 | 79 | 278 | Colombia |
| 0 | 0 | 0 | 0 | 0 | 21 | 6 | 0 | 19 | 10 | 58 | France |
| 72 | 9 | 23 | 1 | 90 | 8 | 0 | 6 | 15 | 4 | 228 | Germany |
| 9 | 1 | 41 | 75 | 5 | 2 | 66 | 11 | 2 | 140 | 351 | Hungary |
| 42 | 22 | 23 | 15 | 30 | 4 | 19 | 24 | 0 | 2 | 182 | India |
| 1 | 110 | 5 | 173 | 17 | 3 | 52 | 33 | 41 | 10 | 446 | Iran |
| 12 | 8 | 2 | 0 | 31 | 1 | 0 | 0 | 3 | 7 | 64 | Italy |
| 29 | 9 | 23 | 5 | 13 | 14 | 209 | 3 | 7 | 27 | 340 | Japan |
| 1 | 43 | 19 | 29 | 65 | 22 | 0 | 10 | 0 | 1 | 190 | Korea |
| 57 | 5 | 51 | 0 | 3 | 13 | 307 | 23 | 3 | 2 | 463 | Malaysia |
| 36 | 2 | 15 | 11 | 74 | 0 | 24 | 11 | 19 | 3 | 196 | Netherlands |
| 3 | 22 | 32 | 0 | 0 | 5 | 128 | 32 | 25 | 46 | 294 | Philippines |
| 29 | 205 | 1 | 31 | 16 | 22 | 0 | 9 | 0 | 34 | 346 | UK |
| 7 | 32 | 1 | 25 | 11 | 1 | 10 | 3 | 0 | 2 | 92 | USA |
| | | | | | | Arithmetic mean | | | | | |
| 25 | 33 | 16 | 27 | 27 | 10 | 59 | 13 | 11 | 26 | 245 | NA |

*Note*: All entries to be divided by 10,000; NA = not applicable
*Source:* Theil et al. (1989), Table 4-4.

cating that the fit for these countries is relatively good. On the other hand, the fit for Malaysia and Iran is much worse than average.

The largest Strobel component of Malaysia is that of Transport and communications (column 7). Turning to the last row of the table we find that this consumption group has the largest average Strobel component over the 15 countries. We also find that besides Malaysia, Japan and the Philippines have large Strobel components for Transport and communications. Could this have something to do with the fact that these countries consist of several islands (Japan and the Philippines) or of an island component and a mainland component (Malaysia)? We shall not answer this question here; it is sufficient to note that Table 4-1 is informative.

## 2. The informational fitting of allocation models

Fitting a model is not exactly the same as the fit of the model, but the two concepts are closely related. We may fit a line or a plane by least squares, and the sum of the squared residuals is a measure of fit. Similarly, when we agree on the use of $I_c$ defined in (1.4) as a measure of fit, we should consider an appropriate extension of $I_c$ as a criterion for estimating the parameters of the model from which we derive the predicted budget shares. Specifically, assume that suitable data exist for $N$ countries ($c = 1, \dots, N$). Let $\theta$ be the parameter vector of the model and write $\hat{w}_{ic}(\theta)$ for the predicted per capita budget share of good $i$ in country $c$ when the model uses $\theta$ as parameter vector. Then

$$I_c(\theta) = \sum_{i=1}^{n} w_{ic} \log[w_{ic}/\hat{w}_{ic}(\theta)] \qquad (2.1)$$

is the information inaccuracy for country $c$ given $\theta$. Naturally, we are interested in minimizing this inaccuracy, at least on the average over the $N$ countries of the sample. Therefore, the MI (minimum information) estimate of $\theta$ is obtained by minimizing

$$\bar{I}(\theta) = (1/N) \sum_{c=1}^{N} I_c(\theta) \qquad (2.2)$$

with respect to $\theta$. Again, we can use the additivity of the information concept to justify the arithmetic mean in (2.2).

We should admit that this idea is not original, not even in demand system estimation. In the latter area four papers were published by Theil, Finke and Flood[1] based on the Addilog and the Rotterdam models. These models are of the time series type, whereas the present article concentrations on cross-

[1] See Theil, Finke and Flood (1984), Finke, Flood and Theil (1984), Flood, Finke and Theil (1984), and Finke and Theil (1984).

country systems. The four papers deal with the efficiency of ML (maximum likelihood), the effect of fat-tailed error distributions, the use of bootstrap replications to approximate standard errors, and other topics.

We should emphasize that the MI approach is not confined to the estimation of consumer demand systems. The crucial consideration is that the dependent variable in each equation is a proportion or a share, and that this share is positive (at least nonnegative) and adds up to 1 when summed over all equations. Such a share may be the budget share of a consumer good, but it may also be an input share of a firm or an import share in international trade. Population shares and income shares are also a possibility. In general, the MI approach is applicable to *allocation models*, but we shall confine ourselves to budget shares of consumer goods in most of what follows.

## 3. Maximum likelihood and its small-sample problems

The application of maximum likelihood (ML) requires a specification of the distribution of the error terms. In most demand systems this amounts to multivariate normality. Returning to the budget share $w_{ic}$, we can write such a specification as

$$w_{ic} = \hat{w}_{ic}(\theta) + \varepsilon_{ic} \tag{3.1}$$

where the error vector $(\varepsilon_{1c}, \varepsilon_{2c}, \ldots)$ is multinormal with zero and covariance matrix $\Omega$. Since $\Omega$ is typically unknown, the ML procedure estimates both $\theta$ and $\Omega$. If $\hat{\theta}$ is the ML estimate of $\theta$, the ML estimate $\hat{\Omega}$ of $\Omega$ is the matrix of mean squares and products of the residuals associated with $\hat{\theta}$.

The ML procedure has well-known optimal properties for large samples under appropriate conditions, but this raises the question: How large is large? It has become increasingly clear in the last few decades that in the case of systems estimation the answer depends on the number of equations. If the sample is sufficiently large, we can approximate $\Omega$ by $\hat{\Omega}$ and apply large-sample results, but doing so becomes dangerous when the model consists of more than a few equations. One danger is that the sampling variances of the ML coefficient estimates increase with the number of equations; the asymptotic variances conceal this unfortunate tendency. Another danger is the fact that likelihood ratio tests reject null hypotheses too frequently.

We shall illustrate this danger by means of simulation experiments conducted by Laitinen (1978) and Meisner (1979). Laitinen considered demand homogeneity; it means that the demand for each good is not affected when income and all prices change proportionately. He used a demand system (the Rotterdam model) which is linear in the parameters; homogeneity then amounts to a zero sum of certain coefficients in each equation. Under normality the standard procedure for testing homogeneity is an $F$ ratio which involves $\Omega$. When we replace $\Omega$ by $\hat{\Omega}$, the test statistic is simplified and has a large-sample chi-square distribution with $n - 1$ degrees of freedom ($n$ = number of goods). Laitinen applied this approximate test to Dutch data published by Theil (1975: 264–265) for 31 annual observations and $n = 14$. He obtained a value of almost 268 for his test statistic, which is obviously unacceptable for a chi-square distribution with 13 degrees of freedom.

Should we conclude that homogeneity is an unacceptable hypothesis for these data? Laitinen decided to pursue this matter by means of a simulation experiment. In this experiment the values of the independent variables of the model (real income and prices) are identical to those of the Dutch data. The true values of the coefficients are specified so that homogeneity is satisfied. Error vectors are drawn from a pseudo-normal distribution with zero mean and a numerically specified covariance matrix $\Omega$. Having drawn such error vectors 31 times (31 = sample size), Laitinen computed the implied values of the dependent variables and then the value of the test statistic. When this is done 100 times, the statistic should be located about five times in the 5 percent rejection region (because the null hypothesis is true by construction). However, the actual results obtained by Laitinen, reproduced in the left half of Table 4-2, show that this hypothesis is far too often rejected. The experiment uses demand systems of different sizes, for $n = 5$, 8, 11 and 14 equations. The table shows that there are too many rejections for each $n$, both at the 5 percent and at the 1 percent level, and that the rejection percentage increases with increasing $n$. The right half of the table concerns the test for Slutsky symmetry; it will be discussed in the paragraph immediately following the next.

A simulation experiment has the advantage that everything is known, including the matrix $\Omega$. Laitinen exploited this feature by computing the $F$ ratio which uses the true $\Omega$ (see the third paragraph of this section). For this ratio the rejection percentages are quite close to the significance level, thus indicating that the $F$ test should work satisfactorily if we could apply it (i.e., if we knew $\Omega$).[2] Evidently, the deficiencies displayed in the left half of

*Table 4-2.* Rejections of homogeneity and symmetry

| | Rejections of homogeneity | | Rejections of symmetry | |
|---|---|---|---|---|
| | 5 percent | 1 percent | 5 percent | 1 percent |
| $n = 5$ | 14 | 6 | 9 | 3 |
| $n = 8$ | 30 | 16 | 26 | 8 |
| $n = 11$ | 53 | 35 | 50 | 37 |
| $n = 14$ | 87 | 81 | 96 | 91 |

*Source:* Theil et al. (1989), Table 3-2.

[2] Laitinen also derived the exact distribution (rather than the asymptotic chi-square distribution) of the test statistic under the null hypothesis of homogeneity. For a sample of size 31 and $n = 14$, the 5 percent critical value (based on the exact distribution) is 306.3. Recall from the end of the third paragraph of this section that the value of the test statistic for the Dutch data is almost 268; hence, this value is not evidence against homogeneity at all.

Table 4-2 indicate that the asymptotic chi-square approximation of the homogeneity test becomes of poorer quality when $n$ increases.

The right half of Table 4-2, from Meisner (1979), gives analogous results for the test of Slutsky symmetry. This property states that the Slutsky coefficient of the $j^{\text{th}}$ price in the demand equation for good $i$ equals the Slutsky coefficient of the $i^{\text{th}}$ price in the $j^{\text{th}}$ equation. The symmetry test also involves $\Omega$; when this is replaced by $\hat{\Omega}$, the test statistic also has an asymptotic chi-square distribution (but with a different number of degrees of freedom). The right half of Table 4-2 indicates that the number of rejections of this asymptotic test is also much too large, particularly for $n = 8$ and larger.

These results strongly suggest that when $\Omega$ is unknown, it has some merits to consider inference methods other than ML. The MI method introduced in Section 2 is one such method. The discussion will continue in Section 6.

## 4. Working's model

In this section and the next we develop the cross-country demand model whose fit is described in Table 4-1 (Section 1). Our starting point in the present section is Working's (1943) model, which is an Engel curve model. Let $M_i$ be the expenditure on good $i$ and $M$ total consumption expenditure ($M = M_1 + \ldots + M_n$). The budget share of good $i$ is then $w_i = M_i/M$. Working's model states

$$w_i = \alpha_i + \beta_i \log M \tag{4.1}$$

where the $\alpha$'s and the $\beta$'s are parameters that are subject to the constraints

$$\sum_{i=1}^{n} \alpha_i = 1 \quad \text{and} \quad \sum_{i=1}^{n} \beta_i = 0 \tag{4.2}$$

We multiply (4.1) by $M$ so that we obtain $w_iM = M_i$ on the left. The result can thus be written as $M_i = \alpha_iM + \beta_iM \log M$, which we differentiate with respect to $M$:

$$\mathrm{d}M_i/\mathrm{d}M = \alpha_i + \beta_i(1 + \log M) = w_i + \beta_i \tag{4.3}$$

where the last step is based on (4.1). The derivative on the left in (4.3) is the marginal budget share of good $i$; we abbreviate this to the *marginal share* of this good. Thus, under Working's model we have the result that the marginal share exceeds the corresponding budget share by the (positive or negative) constant $\beta_i$.

For any Engel curve model, the ratio of the marginal share to the budget share is the income elasticity of the demand for the good (the elasticity with respect to total consumption expenditure). It follows from (4.3) that in the special case of Working's model this elasticity takes the form

$$\text{Income elasticity of good } i = 1 + \beta_i/w_i \tag{4.4}$$

which shows that good $i$ is a luxury (has an income elasticity exceeding 1) if $\beta_i > 0$ and that good $i$ is a necessity (has an income elasticity below 1) if $\beta_i < 0$.

Also, given that the budget share $w_i$ increases with increasing income if $i$ is a luxury ($\beta_i > 0$), we conclude from (4.4) that the income elasticities of luxuries decline toward 1 when income increases. Similarly, given that the budget share of a necessity ($\beta_i < 0$) decreases with increasing income, we conclude from (4.4) that the income elasticities of necessities also decline when income increases. Thus, under Working's model both luxuries and necessities have declining income elasticities.

## 5. The Florida model

Our next step consists of extending Working's model so that it includes the effect of prices. We write $p_{ic}$ for the price of good $i$ the county $c$; see Appendix B for the way in which price data are obtained. We define $\bar{p}_i$ as the geometric mean of the prices of good $i$ in the $N$ countries of the sample:

$$\log \bar{p}_i = (1/N) \sum_{c=1}^{N} \log p_{ic} \tag{5.1}$$

We write $Q_c$ for the volume of total consumption per capita in country $c$; for brevity we shall refer to $Q_c$ as per capita real income. Then, substituting real income $Q_c$ for money income $M$ in (4.1), we conclude from that equation and from (4.3) that the per capita budget and marginal shares of good $i$ in country $c$ can be written as

$$\alpha_i + \beta_i \log Q_c \qquad \text{and} \qquad \alpha_i + \beta_i(1 + \log Q_c)$$

respectively. It will prove convenient to write this as

$$\text{Budget share} = \alpha_i + \beta_i q_c \qquad \text{where} \qquad q_c = \log Q_c \tag{5.2}$$

$$\text{Marginal share} = \alpha_i + \beta_i q_c^* \qquad \text{where} \qquad q_c^* = 1 + q_c \tag{5.3}$$

The observed budget share $w_{ic}$ is not equal to the value shown in (5.2). To formulate Working's model with a fixed set of $\alpha$'s and $\beta$'s we must select a particular set of prices, for which we shall use the geometric means defined in (5.1). The model should then be extended so that it includes the effect on $w_{ic}$ of the fact that the prices in country $c$ pare $p_{1c}, \ldots, p_{nc}$ rather than $\bar{p}_1, \ldots, \bar{p}_n$. This matter is pursued in Appendix C. The model that emerges is polynomial in the parameters,

$$w_{ic} = \text{LINEAR} + \text{QUADRATIC} + \text{CUBIC} + \varepsilon_{ic} \tag{5.4}$$

where $\varepsilon_{ic}$ is a random error term. The linear term is the real-income term, the quadratic term is the "pure" price term, and the cubic term is the substitution term:

$$\text{LINEAR} = \text{Real-income term} = \alpha_i + \beta_i q_c \tag{5.5}$$

QUADRATIC = Pure price term

$$= (\alpha_i + \beta_i q_c)\left[\log\frac{p_{ic}}{\bar{p}_i} - \sum_{j=1}^{n}(\alpha_j + \beta_j q_c)\log\frac{p_{jc}}{\bar{p}_j}\right] \tag{5.6}$$

CUBIC = Substitution term

$$= \phi(\alpha_i + \beta_i q_c^*)\left[\log\frac{p_{ic}}{\bar{p}_i} - \sum_{j=1}^{n}(\alpha_j + \beta_j q_c^*)\log\frac{p_{jc}}{\bar{p}_j}\right] \tag{5.7}$$

On comparing (5.5) with (5.2) we conclude that the linear term is simply the budget share, which is indeed linear in $\alpha_i$ and $\beta_i$. Note that this is the budget share at the real income $Q_c$ and geometric mean prices, because the two other terms (the quadratic and cubic terms) both vanish when the $p_{ic}$'s coincide with the $\bar{p}_i$'s. Actually, for these terms to vanish it is sufficient that the price ratios $p_{ic}/p_{jc}$ coincide with $\bar{p}_i/\bar{p}_j$ (because only relative prices matter).

The reader may be surprised to find that there are two price terms, but a little reflection will convince him that this is a plausible result. The pure price term shown in (5.6) reflects the fact that a higher price $p_{ic}$ raises the expenditure on good $i$ (and hence the budget share $w_{ic}$) when the consumers decide to buy the same quantities in spite of the higher price. The substitution term shown in (5.7) recognizes that the consumers will not buy the same quantities; instead, they react to the higher price by substitution. This substitution term is derived under the simplifying assumption of preference independence; that is, we assume that the consumer's tastes can be represented by a utility function which is additive in the quantities of the $n$ goods. Appendix C provides further details.

The model consisting of equations (5.4) to (5.7) is known as the *Florida model* since Seale et al. (1991); the term used earlier by Theil et al. (1989) is the Working-PI model (PI = preference independence). Note that (5.6) is indeed quadratic in the parameters because it involves squares and products of the $\alpha$'s and $\beta$'s, and that (5.7) is cubic because it involves the parameter $\phi$ also. The reciprocal of this parameter, $1/\phi$, is the income elasticity of the marginal utility of income, which is negative. We shall refer to $\phi$ as the *income flexibility*.

Also note that the expressions in brackets in both (5.6) and (5.7) are deflated logarithmic price ratios $p_{ic}/\bar{p}_i$, the deflators being weighted means of these logarithmic ratios. However, the weights are different. In (5.6) they are the budget shares of (5.2) but in (5.7) they are the marginal shares of (5.3).

## 6. Two methods of estimating the Florida model

We return to the 10 goods mentioned in Section 1 and we use data for 1970 (for the 15 countries listed in the last column of Table 4-1), 1975 (for 30 countries) and 1980 (for 24 countries). The two estimation methods are ML under multinormality and MI; the latter method is distribution-free. (We do assume that the error vectors of different countries are independent.) Both methods require iterations; details are provided in Appendix D.

The ML results are shown in columns 2, 4 and 6 of Table 4-3, and the MI results in columns 3, 5 and 7. All six $\phi$ estimates have the required negative sign. The $\beta_i$'s of Food are close to each other; their negative sign confirms that Food is a necessity. The $\beta_i$'s of three goods (Beverages and tobacco, Clothing and footwear, and Education) have different signs in different columns, which suggests that these goods are close to the borderline between luxuries and necessities. The $\beta_i$'s of the six other goods have the sign of luxury goods.

*Table 4-3.* Data-based estimates for $n = 10$

| | 1970 ($N$ = 15) | | 1975 ($N$ = 30) | | 1980 ($N$ = 24) | |
|---|---|---|---|---|---|---|
| Good (1) | ML (2) | MI (3) | ML (4) | MI (5) | ML (6) | MI (7) |
| | | | Income flexibility $\phi$ | | | |
| NA | −0.747 | −0.647 | −0.511 | −0.526 | −0.625 | −0.651 |
| | | | Coefficients $\beta_i$ | | | |
| 1. Food | −0.154 | −0.147 | −0.145 | −0.145 | −0.140 | −0.140 |
| 2. Beverages, tobacco | 0.004 | 0.001 | 0.004 | 0.000 | −0.003 | −0.005 |
| 3. Clothing, footwear | 0.002 | 0.002 | −0.003 | −0.003 | −0.003 | −0.003 |
| 4. Gross rent, fuel | 0.027 | 0.026 | 0.029 | 0.030 | 0.030 | 0.024 |
| 5. House furnishings[a] | 0.021 | 0.026 | 0.025 | 0.026 | 0.017 | 0.018 |
| 6. Medical care | 0.023 | 0.023 | 0.026 | 0.023 | 0.029 | 0.026 |
| 7. Transport[b] | 0.030 | 0.019 | 0.027 | 0.027 | 0.032 | 0.028 |
| 8. Recreation | 0.024 | 0.024 | 0.020 | 0.019 | 0.012 | 0.016 |
| 9. Education | 0.005 | −0.000 | −0.014 | −0.010 | −0.005 | 0.006 |
| 10. Other | 0.018 | 0.026 | 0.031 | 0.033 | 0.032 | 0.031 |
| | | | Coefficients $\alpha_i$ | | | |
| 1. Food | 0.137 | 0.144 | 0.163 | 0.164 | 0.171 | 0.172 |
| 2. Beverages, tobacco | 0.063 | 0.059 | 0.060 | 0.056 | 0.054 | 0.052 |
| 3. Clothing, footwear | 0.088 | 0.089 | 0.084 | 0.084 | 0.077 | 0.077 |
| 4. Gross rent, fuel | 0.154 | 0.152 | 0.145 | 0.145 | 0.145 | 0.141 |
| 5. House furnishings[a] | 0.096 | 0.101 | 0.097 | 0.098 | 0.084 | 0.085 |
| 6. Medical care | 0.088 | 0.087 | 0.093 | 0.090 | 0.091 | 0.089 |
| 7. Transport[b] | 0.117 | 0.107 | 0.115 | 0.115 | 0.128 | 0.126 |
| 8. Recreation | 0.074 | 0.075 | 0.069 | 0.068 | 0.064 | 0.066 |
| 9. Education | 0.067 | 0.062 | 0.050 | 0.053 | 0.059 | 0.065 |
| 10. Other | 0.116 | 0.124 | 0.124 | 0.126 | 0.127 | 0.126 |

NA = not applicable.
[a] House furnishings and operations.
[b] Transport and communications.

When we make a pairwise comparison of columns 2–3, and similarly for columns 4–5 and 6–7, it becomes evident that the largest pairwise differences are those between columns 2 and 3. This should come as no surprise, given that these columns are based on the smallest number of observations (15 countries). For example, the ML and MI estimates of $\phi$ in columns 2 and 3 differ by 0.1, whereas the two other differences in the same row are smaller than 0.03. Which method yields better results, ML or MI?

## 7. A simulation experiment

We shall try to answer this question by means of a simulation experiment (similar to Table 4-2 in Section 3). The simulation design uses true values of the coefficients (the $\alpha$'s, $\beta$'s and $\phi$) and of the covariance matrix $\Omega$ which are all the same for the three years 1970, 1975 and 1980. The true values of the coefficients, shown in column 2 of Table 4-4, are combined with the data-based values of the independent variables (the $p_{ic}$'s and $q_c$'s) and pseudo-normal error vectors (with zero mean and covariance matrix $\Omega$). This yields a pseudo-sample of size 15 for 1970, 30 for 1975, and 24 for 1980, which was repeated 100 times independently and then 1000 times.

We can thus obtain 100 or 1000 estimates for our two estimation methods (ML and MI). Actually, we shall use two ML methods: ML with unknown $\Omega$ (MLU for short) and ML with known $\Omega$ (MLK); this is possible in a simulation experiment because its $\Omega$ is known. Thus, we obtain 100 or 1000 estimates for three methods: MLU, MLK and MI. The arithmetic means of these estimates (not shown here) are all close to the true value; bias does not appear to be much of a problem. The RMSEs (root-mean-square errors) around the true value are shown in the last nine columns of Table 4-4 for the 1000 trials. Note the sizeable difference between columns 3 and 4; not knowing $\Omega$ raises the RMSEs of the ML estimates substantially for $N = 15$. A comparison with column 5 shows that the MI approach is far superior to MLU.

A similar pattern, but with smaller differences, is visible in the last three columns of the table ($N = 24$). For $N = 30$ (in 1975) the difference is still smaller, but it remains noticeable for $\phi$. It seems that we must conclude that when the sample is small and when $\Omega$ is unknown (as it usually is), the MI approach is preferable to ML.

## 8. An extension involving the demand for energy

Before we actually draw this conclusion we should explore the effect of the number of equations ($n$). Recall that the Laitinen-Meisner experiments summarized in Table 4-2 (Section 3) reveal that the deficiencies of the large-sample homogeneity and symmetry tests become more serious when $n$ increases. We

*Table 4-4.* A simulation experiment for $n = 10$

| | | RMSE around the true value | | | | | | | | |
|---|---|---|---|---|---|---|---|---|---|---|
| | | 1970 ($N = 15$) | | | 1975 ($N = 30$) | | | 1980 ($N = 24$) | | |
| $i$ | True value | MLU | MLK | MI | MLU | MLK | MI | MLU | MLK | MI |
| (1) | (2) | (3) | (4) | (5) | (6) | (7) | (8) | (9) | (10) | (11) |
| | | | | | Income flexibility $\phi$ | | | | | |
| NA | −5694 | 1768 | 843 | 984 | 577 | 475 | 546 | 628 | 461 | 510 |
| | | | | | Coefficients $\beta_i$ | | | | | |
| 1 | −1377 | 363 | 135 | 140 | 104 | 102 | 105 | 118 | 107 | 113 |
| 2 | 1 | 135 | 60 | 61 | 51 | 49 | 50 | 53 | 49 | 51 |
| 3 | −55 | 120 | 53 | 54 | 45 | 42 | 43 | 45 | 40 | 42 |
| 4 | 241 | 255 | 74 | 77 | 60 | 58 | 61 | 68 | 61 | 64 |
| 5 | 180 | 138 | 61 | 65 | 45 | 43 | 45 | 46 | 41 | 43 |
| 6 | 193 | 135 | 60 | 61 | 47 | 45 | 47 | 64 | 56 | 64 |
| 7 | 323 | 206 | 81 | 82 | 72 | 68 | 72 | 83 | 76 | 81 |
| 8 | 174 | 128 | 43 | 45 | 34 | 33 | 35 | 42 | 37 | 39 |
| 9 | 24 | 227 | 104 | 112 | 102 | 91 | 97 | 137 | 107 | 116 |
| 10 | 296 | 222 | 85 | 89 | 68 | 66 | 69 | 58 | 52 | 56 |
| | | | | | Coefficients $\alpha_i$ | | | | | |
| 1 | 1718 | 566 | 185 | 191 | 122 | 122 | 124 | 108 | 106 | 109 |
| 2 | 562 | 185 | 96 | 98 | 68 | 67 | 68 | 62 | 61 | 62 |
| 3 | 810 | 159 | 74 | 75 | 52 | 50 | 51 | 47 | 46 | 46 |
| 4 | 1419 | 439 | 109 | 111 | 75 | 74 | 76 | 71 | 69 | 71 |
| 5 | 893 | 204 | 82 | 86 | 54 | 53 | 55 | 49 | 47 | 49 |
| 6 | 845 | 176 | 82 | 83 | 56 | 54 | 56 | 53 | 50 | 54 |
| 7 | 1226 | 338 | 117 | 119 | 83 | 82 | 84 | 77 | 75 | 78 |
| 8 | 656 | 190 | 62 | 65 | 43 | 42 | 43 | 38 | 37 | 37 |
| 9 | 635 | 246 | 112 | 119 | 93 | 83 | 88 | 90 | 74 | 78 |
| 10 | 1236 | 437 | 114 | 117 | 79 | 78 | 80 | 65 | 63 | 65 |

NA = not applicable; MLU = ML, unknown $\Omega$; MLK = ML, known $\Omega$.
*Note:* All entries to be divided by 10,000.

shall explore the effect of $n$ here by taking the energy components out of two of the $n$ goods and creating a separate good called Energy (see Appendix B for further details). Thus, we increase $n = 10$ to $n = 11$.

Table 4-5, which should be compared with Table 4-3 (Section 6), shows the results of ML and MI approaches to the Florida model when applied to these 11 goods; Energy is listed here as the fifth good. Note that the ML approach fails to converge for $N = 15$. This approach uses the inverse of the estimate of $\Omega$ in each iteration. For $N = 15$ the successive iterated values of this estimate tend to become more and more ill-conditioned.

Again, a simulation experiment is instructive. Its design is similar to that of Table 4-4 except that we now have 11 goods. Another difference is that

*Table 4-5.* Data-based estimates for $n = 11$

| | 1970 ($N$ = 15) | | 1975 ($N$ = 30) | | 1980 ($N$ = 24) | |
|---|---|---|---|---|---|---|
| Good<br>(1) | ML<br>(2) | MI<br>(3) | ML<br>(4) | MI<br>(5) | ML<br>(6) | MI<br>(7) |
| | | Income inflexibility $\phi$ | | | | |
| NA | NC | –0.655 | –0.515 | –0.520 | –0.616 | –0.650 |
| | | Coefficients $\beta_i$ | | | | |
| 1. Food | NC | –0.148 | –0.146 | –0.145 | –0.141 | –0.141 |
| 2. Beverages, tobacco | NC | 0.001 | 0.004 | 0.001 | –0.003 | –0.005 |
| 3. Clothing, footwear | NC | 0.002 | –0.003 | –0.003 | –0.003 | –0.003 |
| 4. Gross rent, fuel | NC | 0.029 | 0.028 | 0.027 | 0.025 | 0.020 |
| 5. Energy | NC | 0.010 | 0.014 | 0.014 | 0.019 | 0.017 |
| 6. House furnishings[a] | NC | 0.025 | 0.025 | 0.026 | 0.017 | 0.018 |
| 7. Medical care | NC | 0.023 | 0.026 | 0.023 | 0.027 | 0.026 |
| 8. Transport[b] | NC | 0.011 | 0.016 | 0.016 | 0.019 | 0.017 |
| 9. Recreation | NC | 0.024 | 0.019 | 0.019 | 0.011 | 0.016 |
| 10. Education | NC | –0.001 | –0.013 | –0.011 | –0.004 | 0.005 |
| 11. Other | NC | 0.025 | 0.031 | 0.033 | 0.032 | 0.031 |
| | | Coefficients $\alpha_i$ | | | | |
| 1. Food | NC | 0.143 | 0.162 | 0.164 | 0.168 | 0.169 |
| 2. Beverages, tobacco | NC | 0.059 | 0.060 | 0.057 | 0.054 | 0.052 |
| 3. Clothing, footwear | NC | 0.087 | 0.084 | 0.084 | 0.076 | 0.076 |
| 4. Gross rent, fuel | NC | 0.124 | 0.107 | 0.106 | 0.107 | 0.103 |
| 5. Energy | NC | 0.059 | 0.067 | 0.066 | 0.076 | 0.074 |
| 6. House furnishings[a] | NC | 0.100 | 0.097 | 0.098 | 0.085 | 0.086 |
| 7. Medical care | NC | 0.087 | 0.093 | 0.090 | 0.091 | 0.090 |
| 8. Transport[b] | NC | 0.082 | 0.087 | 0.088 | 0.094 | 0.094 |
| 9. Recreation | NC | 0.075 | 0.069 | 0.068 | 0.063 | 0.065 |
| 10. Education | NC | 0.061 | 0.051 | 0.053 | 0.061 | 0.066 |
| 11. Other | NC | 0.123 | 0.124 | 0.126 | 0.126 | 0.125 |

NA = not applicable; NC = no convergence.
[a] House furnishings and operations.
[b] Transport and communications.

we reject pseudo-normal error drawings ($\varepsilon_{ic}$) which imply a negative pseudo-observed budget share ($w_{ic}$); hence, the drawings are now from a truncated multinormal distribution. Further details are provided in Appendix D. The RMSEs based on 1000 trials are shown in Table 4-6. Note the NCs in column 2; they mean that for $N$ = 15 (in 1970) the ML procedure with unknown $\Omega$ fails to converge in a large majority of the 1000 trials. On the other hand, columns 3 and 4 show that for this $N$ the RMSEs of the MI estimates are not much larger than those of the ML estimates with known $\Omega$. The last six columns of the table show results close to those of the corresponding columns of Table 4-4. The MI approach is clearly superior to ML with unknown $\Omega$ when

*Table 4-6.* A simulation experiment for $n = 11$

| | RMSE around the true value | | | | | | | | |
|---|---|---|---|---|---|---|---|---|---|
| | 1970 ($N = 15$) | | | 1975 ($N = 30$) | | | 1980 ($N = 24$) | | |
| $i$ | MLU | MLK | MI | MLU | MLK | MI | MLU | MLK | MI |
| (1) | (2) | (3) | (4) | (5) | (6) | (7) | (8) | (9) | (10) |
| | | | | Income flexibility $\phi$ | | | | | |
| NA | NC | 749 | 831 | 546 | 436 | 488 | 611 | 433 | 487 |
| | | | | Coefficients $\beta_i$ | | | | | |
| 1 | NC | 128 | 131 | 103 | 96 | 99 | 122 | 107 | 113 |
| 2 | NC | 60 | 61 | 50 | 46 | 48 | 52 | 48 | 49 |
| 3 | NC | 52 | 54 | 43 | 40 | 42 | 44 | 39 | 40 |
| 4 | NC | 68 | 71 | 55 | 51 | 53 | 61 | 52 | 55 |
| 5 | NC | 44 | 47 | 37 | 35 | 36 | 45 | 38 | 40 |
| 6 | NC | 59 | 62 | 43 | 42 | 44 | 45 | 41 | 44 |
| 7 | NC | 59 | 60 | 46 | 44 | 45 | 66 | 55 | 62 |
| 8 | NC | 72 | 74 | 61 | 57 | 59 | 75 | 66 | 68 |
| 9 | NC | 40 | 40 | 33 | 31 | 34 | 40 | 36 | 38 |
| 10 | NC | 95 | 100 | 98 | 85 | 91 | 146 | 107 | 116 |
| 11 | NC | 86 | 90 | 69 | 66 | 69 | 58 | 52 | 56 |
| | | | | Coefficients $\alpha_i$ | | | | | |
| 1 | NC | 176 | 179 | 120 | 117 | 120 | 113 | 111 | 113 |
| 2 | NC | 93 | 94 | 62 | 61 | 62 | 61 | 60 | 60 |
| 3 | NC | 77 | 79 | 52 | 50 | 52 | 46 | 45 | 46 |
| 4 | NC | 100 | 102 | 68 | 65 | 66 | 63 | 60 | 62 |
| 5 | NC | 71 | 74 | 48 | 47 | 48 | 48 | 46 | 47 |
| 6 | NC | 80 | 83 | 55 | 54 | 56 | 48 | 47 | 48 |
| 7 | NC | 76 | 78 | 52 | 51 | 53 | 53 | 49 | 52 |
| 8 | NC | 101 | 102 | 72 | 70 | 71 | 69 | 66 | 67 |
| 9 | NC | 61 | 61 | 41 | 40 | 42 | 39 | 38 | 39 |
| 10 | NC | 106 | 110 | 88 | 78 | 84 | 87 | 68 | 73 |
| 11 | NC | 118 | 121 | 80 | 78 | 80 | 66 | 64 | 67 |

NA = not applicable; NC = no convergence.
*Note:* All entries to be divided by 10,000.

$N$ is small. Deleting drawings that yield negative pseudo-observed budget shares has no noticeable effect.

## 9. An informational approach to outlier analysis

In the previous sections we used data for 15 countries in 1970, 30 countries in 1975 and 24 countries in 1980. Actually, data are available for more countries. Fourteen country-year pairs have been identified as outliers on the basis of the information inaccuracy criterion $I_c$ defined in (1.4). These countries are listed in alphabetical order in column 1 of Table 4-7; note that they are all in Africa and Middle America (Central America and West Indies). The $I_c$'s are shown in column 2. In one case (Malawi in 1980) $I_c$ cannot be computed because the $\hat{w}_{ic}$ of Transport and communications is negative. It follows from (1.4) that if $w_{ic} > 0$ and $\hat{w}_{ic}$ declines from a small positive value toward zero, $I_c$ increases beyond bounds; a negative $\hat{w}_{ic}$ is obviously even worse than a zero $\hat{w}_{ic}$.

We suspected that an important cause of outliers is the artificially low value of food consumption in a number of poor countries. Specifically, when we plot the budget share of food against the logarithm of total real per capita consumption expenditure (Working's model), we find that the outliers are poor countries (but not all poor countries are outliers) and that the food budget shares of these outliers are too low. It seems reasonable to relate this to the fact that in the rural areas and small towns of underdeveloped countries there are many poor households which grow their own food on their own plots of land. This agricultural production does not reach the marketplace. Statisticians do try to estimate this production, but it seems reasonable to guess that (at least for some of these countries) this production will be underestimated. The remainder of this section is an attempt to verify this proposition.

In column 3 of Table 4-7 we act as if food consumption is 25 percent higher than reported; in columns 4 to 6 we double this percentage successively. Take Cameroon in 1980 as an example (the first row of the table). Its food

*Table 4-7.* Information inaccuracies for outliers

| | Inaccuracy ($\times 10^4$) when food expenditure is raised by | | | | |
|---|---|---|---|---|---|
| Country, year (1) | 0% (2) | 25% (3) | 50% (4) | 100% (5) | 200% (6) |
| Cameroon, 1980 | 2208 | 1603 | 1176 | 677 | 455 |
| Ethiopia, 1980 | 3121 | 2281 | 1693 | 1000 | 607 |
| Guatemala, 1980 | 1281 | 1119 | 1103 | 1323 | 2175 |
| Honduras, 1980 | 1201 | 896 | 759 | 779 | 1339 |
| Ivory Coast, 1980 | 1170 | 893 | 805 | 951 | 1778 |
| Jamaica, 1975 | 718 | 604 | 630 | 926 | 1942 |
| Kenya, 1970 | 880 | 547 | 454 | 647 | 1587 |
| Kenya, 1975 | 774 | 418 | 259 | 285 | 933 |
| Kenya, 1980 | 812 | 457 | 296 | 311 | 919 |
| Malawi, 1975 | 654 | 580 | 715 | 1260 | 2618 |
| Malawi, 1980 | NC | 482 | 482 | 894 | 2120 |
| Mali, 1980 | 2870 | 2244 | 1995 | 2015 | 2732 |
| Zambia, 1975 | 917 | 607 | 508 | 669 | 1581 |
| Zimbabwe, 1980 | 3006 | 2364 | 1889 | 1289 | 901 |

*Source:* Theil et al. (1989), Table 4-6.
NC = not computed (see text).

budget share $w_{ic}$ ($i = 1$ for food, $c$ = Cameroon) is obtained by dividing the food expenditure in national currency by total consumption in that currency. If the actual food consumption exceeds the reported consumption by 25 percent, as we assume in column 3, the implied actual *total* consumption exceeds the corresponding reported total by the same amount (because the consumption of all goods other than food remains unchanged). The implication is that when we move from left to right in any row of Table 4-7, the budget share $w_{1c}$ of food increases and that the $w_{ic}$ of any other good ($i \neq 1$) decreases.

But it is not only the observed $w_{ic}$'s that change; it holds for the fitted values $\hat{w}_{ic}$ also. To see this we must consider the independent variables of the demand system: real income and relative prices. We shall argue in the next paragraph that during the move from left to right in each row of Table 4-7, the fitted budget share $\hat{w}_{ic}$ increases when $i$ is a luxury and decreases when $i$ is a necessity. Since food is a necessity, its fitted budget share $\hat{w}_{1c}$ decreases whereas (see the previous paragraph) the observed share $w_{1c}$ increases.

The behavior of the $\hat{w}_{ic}$'s of luxuries and necessities is based on the assumption that when actual food consumption in national currency exceeds the corresponding reported consumption by a certain percentage, the same percentage excess applies to food consumption in real terms. Therefore, the price of food does not change when we move form left to right in any row of Table 4-7 (nor does the price of any other good change), but per capita real income increases. Returning to the three components of the Florida model shown in equations (5.5) to (5.7), we conclude that only the real-income component is affected. It is then easily seen that $\hat{w}_{ic}$ goes up if $\beta_i > 0$ (luxury) and goes down if $\beta_i < 0$ (necessity).

A comparison of columns 2 and 3 of Table 4-7 shows that a 25 percent increase in food consumption improves the fit in all cases. Next, by comparing columns 3 and 4 we find that a 50 percent increase yields a better fit than a 25 percent increase in a substantial majority of all cases. In the subsequent columns this majority becomes minority, but there are still three cases (Cameroon, Ethiopia and Zimbabwe, all in 1980) in which tripling food consumption pays off. Clearly, the fit of the outliers can be improved (sometimes substantially) by assuming that food consumption exceeds what is reported.

## 10. Suggestions for further research

In the previous pages we did not discuss standard errors. Perhaps the reader may think that ML (in contrast to MI) has the advantage of yielding asymptotic standard errors. However, these asymptotic standard errors are notoriously unreliable, particularly when the number of equations ($n$) is not small; these standard errors tend to underestimate the true variability of the ML point estimates considerably. A more promising procedure is to compute bootstrap standard errors, which can be done both for ML and for MI estimates. Finke,

Flood and Theil (1984) and Finke and Theil (1984) applied this procedure to demand systems based on time series data; cross-country applications have not yet been made.

Another possible extension consists of an autoregressive process applied to the cross-country data of 1970, 1975 and 1980. Theil et al. (1989, Sec. 3.4) applied this idea in order to take account of persistent differences in consumer tastes across countries. Their procedure is ML; the corresponding extension for MI has not yet been made. The same holds for the heteroskedastic extension in Theil et al. (1989, Sec. 4.2).

The income flexibility $\phi$ presents an interesting statistical problem. When we compare the row of $\phi$ in Tables 4-4 and 4-6 with the rows for the other parameters, we must conclude that the MLU results for 1975 ($N = 30$) are much worse than for the $\alpha$'s and $\beta$'s. In other words, $\phi$ has the most serious convergence problem among the parameters of the Florida model. It is perhaps possible to obtain more insight into this matter by considering the Divisia and Frisch price variances described in Chapter 5.

## APPENDIX A

### Elements of statistical information theory

*The information concept*

Let $E$ be an event with probability $y$. At some point in time we receive a reliable message stating that $E$ has in fact occurred. The question is: How much information is contained in this message? Note that the nature of $E$ plays no role in this question.

Since the question is vague, we proceed along intuitive lines. Let $y$ be close to 1; say, $y = 0.98$. It is then quite likely that $E$ will take place even before the message arrives, which means that the message is not very informative. On the other hand, let $y$ be close to zero; say $y = 0.01$. If a message arrives stating that $E$ occurred in spite of this low probability (remember that the message is reliable by assumption!), then we are greatly surprised and, hence, the message is quite informative.

These considerations suggest that if our objective is to measure the information content of such a message in terms of the probability $y$ of the event that prevailed prior to the arrival of the message, we should select a *decreasing* function: the more unlikely the event was before the message arrived, the more informative the message is. The function used in statistical information theory since Shannon (1948) is

$$h(y) = -\log y \tag{A1}$$

which decreases from $\infty$ (at $y = 0$) to 0 (at $y = 1$).

The reason for choosing the form (A1) is its additivity for stochastically independent events. Let $E$ and $E^*$ be two events with probabilities $y$ and $y^*$, respectively, and let them be stochastically independent so that the probability if their joint occurrence is $yy^*$. Using (A1), we conclude that the information of the message stating that both $E$ and $E^*$ occurred is

$$h(yy^*) = -\log(yy^*) = -\log y - \log y^*$$

which equals $h(y) + h(y^*)$; that is, this "joint" information is equal to the information of the message on $E$ only plus that of the message on $E^*$ only. Indeed, we can derive (A1) as the unique solution of certain axioms (unique up to the choice of the logarithmic base), the main axiom being that of additivity; see, e.g., Theil et al. (1989), Appendix H3.

*The entropy*

Next consider a complete system of mutually exclusive events, $E_1, \ldots, E_n$ with probabilities $y_1, \ldots, y_n$. If a message arrives stating that $E_i$ occurred, the information received is $h(y_i) = -\log y_i$. Before the message arrives we do not know which $E_i$ will occur, but we do know that its probability is $y_i$.

Therefore, the expected information computed prior to the arrival of the message is

$$H = -\sum_{i=1}^{n} y_i \log y_i \tag{A2}$$

which is also known as the *entropy* of the distribution whose probabilities are $y_1, \ldots, y_n$.

The entropy is nonnegative. The minimum is zero, which occurs when one of the $n$ events has unit probability (and, hence, all others have zero probability). The maximum of $H$ is $\log n$, which occurs when all probabilities are $1/n$. The entropy can be used as a dispersion or uncertainty measure for random variables which take nonnumerical values.

### *A nondefinitive message*

Consider again event $E$ with probability $y$, but assume now that a message arrives stating that the odds in favor of $E$ have changed so that its probability is $z$ rather than $y$. This includes the message of the first subsection as a special case for $z = 1$. We shall refer to $y$ as the *prior probability* of $E$ (prior to the arrival of the message) and to $z$ as the *posterior probability* of $E$. Again, we ask how we can measure the information content of the message, but this is now the message which transforms prior $y$ to posterior $z$.

We shall answer this question under the assumption that $E$ ultimately does occur. The starting point is the prior probability $y$; the end point is the certainty (probability 1) that $E$ occurs. Between these two points *two alternative routes* will be considered: one in which the above-mentioned message is received (transforming $y$ into $z$) followed by a second message that transforms $z$ into 1; and another route in which $y$ is transformed into 1 without intermediate step. Since the initial situation (probability $y$) and the eventual situation (probability 1) are the same for the two routes, we shall require that they contain the same total amount of information. This condition is in the spirit of the additivity of the information concept.

The information conveyed by the second (direct) route is $h(y) = -\log y$. The total information provided by the first route equals the information of the message that transforms $y$ into $z$, plus $h(z)$. Therefore, the information content of the message that transforms prior $y$ into $z$ equals

$$h(y) - h(z) = \log \frac{z}{y} \tag{A3}$$

but note that the underlying arguments involve the assumption that $E$ ultimately occurs. If it turns out that $E$ failed to occur at the end, we can apply the same argument to not-$E$. This amounts to replacing $y$ by $1 - y$ and $z$ by $1 - z$ in (A3):

$$h(1 - y) - h(1 - z) = \log \frac{1 - z}{1 - y} \tag{A4}$$

Therefore, the information of the message that transforms prior $y$ into posterior $z$ is either (A3) or (A4) depending on whether $E$ will ultimately occur or not. Since the message that transforms $y$ into $z$ states that $E$ has probability $z$, its expected information is therefore

$$I = z \log \frac{z}{y} + (1 - z) \log \frac{1 - z}{1 - y} \tag{A5}$$

More generally, consider a complete system of $n$ mutually exclusive events with the prior and posterior probabilities shown below.

| | | |
|---|---|---|
| Events: | $E_1$ | $E_2 \ldots E_n$ |
| Prior: | $y_1$ | $y_2 \ldots y_n$ |
| Posterior: | $z_1$ | $z_2 \ldots z_n$ |

If it turns out that $E_i$ ultimately occurs, the information of the message that transforms the $y$'s into the $z$'s equals $\log(z_i/y_i)$. Since this message states that $E_i$ has probability $z_i$, its expected information is

$$I = \sum_{i=1}^{n} z_i \log (z_i/y_i) \tag{A6}$$

This $I$ is nonnegative; it vanishes if and only if the probabilities are pairwise equal: $y_i = z_i$ for each $i$.

*Applications and extensions*

The information inaccuracy defined in (1.4) is one application of (A6), with the fitted budget share $\hat{w}_{ic}$ playing the role of the prior probability $y_i$ and the observed share $w_{ic}$ that of the posterior probability $z_i$. Note that such shares should add up to 1 *exactly*; if either set of shares fails to add up to 1, serious numerical discrepancies are possible.

There are numerous other applications both of (A2) and of (A6). The entropy of the budget shares is a measure of the diversity of the consumer's basket; see Theil and Clements (1987), Section 2.16. The entropy of the relative Strobel measures $I_{1c}/I_c, \ldots, I_{nc}/I_c$ takes as small value when the lack of fit an allocation model must be attributed mainly to one equation or to a few equations, but it takes a large value when more than a few equations are jointly responsible for the lack of fit; see Theil and Clements (1987), Section 3.16. The information expectation (A6) becomes a measure of income inequality when the two sets of probabilities are population and income shares.

The additivity of the information concept is the primary cause of the attractiveness of these applications. An additional implication of this additivity is the simplicity of the aggregation (between and within groups of events) of both (A2) and (A6); see Theil et al. (1989), Appendix H6.

## APPENDIX B

### Description of the data

*The data for ten goods*

The data are given in Theil et al. (1989), Chapter 1. A brief description follows here.

The origin of the data is the International Comparison Project (ICP) at the University of Pennsylvania. The ICP procedure consists of two steps. Each country's GDP is divided into more than 100 detailed categories, such as fresh vegetables, and each such category consists of a number of items for which prices are available (such as artichokes and beets in the case of fresh vegetables). The first step of the ICP procedure describes the logarithm of the price of such an item in each country as the sum of an item effect and a country effect. The antilog of the country effect is an estimated purchasing power parity (PPP) of the detailed category (fresh vegetables in this case).

By dividing the per capita expenditure in national currency on such a detailed category by this PPP we obtain per capita expenditure in real terms, but such ratios are not additive across categories. To achieve additivity, the ICP uses a second step proposed by Geary (1958) and Khamis (1967, 1970, 1972). This step introduces an overall PPP for each country; "overall" means that this PPP applies to all detailed categories. It also introduces an international price for each detailed category; such a price applies to all countries. For more details we refer to Kravis et al. (1975, 1978, 1982).

The result is that for each detailed category in each country we have two per capita expenditures: in national currency and at international prices. The ratio of the former to the latter is the price of the detailed category in that country. The data for the 10 consumption groups are obtained by straightforward aggregation.

*The energy data*

Two of the 10 goods contain energy components. Transport and communications includes gasoline, grease and oil; Gross rent and fuel includes electricity, gas, liquid and other fuels, water charges and ice. The energy budget shares for India, Korea and Colombia in 1975 and for Korea, Pakistan and Sri Lanka in 1980 may be somewhat underestimated because of missing data for gasoline, grease and oil. However, these observations are broadly consistent with the main tendency in the data.

## APPENDIX C

### Elements of utility theory

*Maximizing utility*

We write $\mathrm{d}u/\mathrm{d}q$ for the vector of first-order derivatives of the consumer's utility function $u(q)$. We assume that these derivatives are all positive in the relevant region (nonsatiation). We write $U = \mathrm{d}^2u/\mathrm{d}q\mathrm{d}q'$ for the Hessian matrix of the utility function. We assume that $U$ is symmetric negative definitive (generalized diminishing marginal utility).

The consumer's objective is to maximize $u(q)$ subject to the budget constraints $p'q = M$ for given positive prices $p' = [p_1 \ldots p_n]$ and income $M$. For this purpose we form the Lagrangian expression $u(q) - \lambda(p'q - M)$, where $\lambda$ is a Lagrangian multiplier. We differentiate this expression with respect to $q$,

$$\mathrm{d}u/\mathrm{d}q = \lambda p \tag{C1}$$

which is the familiar proportionality of the marginal utilities and prices. This proportionality and the budget constraint constitute the first-order condition of the constrained utility maximum. The second-order condition is satisfied by the assumption of a negative definitive Hessian $U$.

The $i^{\text{th}}$ equation of the proportionality (C1) states that the marginal utility of good $i$ equals $\lambda p_i$. On dividing both sides of this equation by $p_i$, we conclude that the marginal utility of a dollar spent on $i$ equals $\lambda$ (independent of $i$). Hence, a one-dollar increase in income causes utility to rise by $\lambda$ when this increase is spent on any of the $n$ goods. Accordingly, $\lambda$ is known as the *marginal utility of income.*

*The income and price derivatives of demand*

When we combine (C1) with the budget constraint $p'q = M$, we have $n + 1$ equations in $n + 1$ unknowns: the $n$ elements of $q$ and $\lambda$. The next step is to differentiate these $n + 1$ equations with respect to the $n + 1$ independent variables: the $n$ elements of $p$ and $M$. This is a matter of applying the chain rule. For example, when differentiating (C1) with respect to $M$, we differentiate the left side with respect to each element of $q'$ (which yields the Hessian $U$) and then differentiate $q'$ with respect to $M$. When this is done diligently, we obtain a result that can be conveniently written in partitioned matrix form:

$$\begin{bmatrix} U & p \\ p' & 0 \end{bmatrix} \begin{bmatrix} \mathrm{d}q/\mathrm{d}M & \mathrm{d}q/\mathrm{d}p' \\ -\mathrm{d}\lambda/\mathrm{d}M & -\mathrm{d}\lambda/\mathrm{d}p' \end{bmatrix} = \begin{bmatrix} 0 & \lambda I \\ 1 & -q' \end{bmatrix} \tag{C2}$$

The matrix on the far left, which is square of order $n + 1$, is the bordered Hessian matrix of the utility function (bordered by prices). The matrix immediately to the left of equal sign is also square of order $n + 1$; it contains the derivatives of all dependent variables ($q$ and $\lambda$) with respect to all independent variables ($p$ and $M$). The reader may want to consult Theil et al. (1989, App. B) for intermediate steps.

To solve (C2) for the income and price derivatives we must premultiply this equation by the inverse of the bordered Hessian on the far left. It may be verified that this yields

$$\mathrm{d}q/\mathrm{d}M = (1/p'U^{-1}p)U^{-1}p, \quad \mathrm{d}\lambda/\mathrm{d}M = 1/p'U^{-1}p \tag{C3}$$

$$\mathrm{d}q/\mathrm{d}p' = \lambda U^{-1} - (\lambda/p'U^{-1}p)U^{-1}p(U^{-1}p)' - (1/p'U^{-1}p)U^{-1}pq' \tag{C4}$$

On combining (C3) and (C4) we conclude that the latter equation can also be written as

$$\mathrm{d}q/\mathrm{d}p' = \lambda U^{-1} - \phi M(\mathrm{d}q/\mathrm{d}M)(\mathrm{d}q/\mathrm{d}M)' - (\mathrm{d}q/\mathrm{d}M)q' \tag{C5}$$

where $\phi$ is the income flexibility; its reciprocal, $1/\phi$, is the income elasticity of $\lambda$.

*Preference independence*

We say that the consumer's tastes are preference independent when they can be represented by a utility function which is additive in the $n$ goods:

$$u(q) = \sum_{i=1}^{n} u_i(q_i) \tag{C6}$$

Under this condition the marginal utilities take the form $\mathrm{d}u_i/\mathrm{d}q_i$, which depends only on the quantity $q_i$. Hence the Hessian $U$ and its inverse become diagonal matrices, so that the first term on the right in (C5) diagonal also.

The latter diagonality has an important simplifying effect on the substitution term. Let $w_i = p_iq_i/M$ be the budget share of good $i$. Then, using (C3) and (C5) we can obtain a differential demand equation of the following form under preference independence:

$$\begin{aligned} w_i\,\mathrm{d}(\log q_i) = {} & \theta_i[\mathrm{d}(\log M) - \mathrm{d}(\log P)] \\ & + \phi\theta_i[\mathrm{d}(\log p_i) - \mathrm{d}(\log P^*)] \end{aligned} \tag{C7}$$

Here $\theta_i = \mathrm{d}(p_iq_i)/\mathrm{d}M$ is the marginal share of good $i$, while $\mathrm{d}(\log P)$ and $\mathrm{d}(\log P^*)$ are the Divisia and Frisch price indices:

$$\mathrm{d}(\log P) = \sum_{i=1}^{n} w_i\mathrm{d}(\log p_i), \quad \mathrm{d}(\log P^*) = \sum_{i=1}^{n} \theta_i\mathrm{d}(\log p_i) \tag{C8}$$

The Divisia index in (C7) results from the third term on the right in (C5) and the Frisch index results from the second, while the first term in (C5) yields the $\mathrm{d}(\log \mathrm{p_i})$ inside the second pair of brackets in (C7). Thus, we have only one logarithmic price change in (C7), apart from the Divisia and Frisch indices. This simplicity results from the assumption of preference independence.

Note that the $\theta_i$'s in (C7) and (C8) are not necessarily constant. In fact, they depend on the income level under the Florida model because this model is based on Working's model (see Section 4).

*The Florida model*

To complete the Florida model we recall from Section 5 that Working's model is postulated to hold with fixed $\alpha$'s and $\beta$'s at the geometric mean prices. So we must extent the model such that it includes the effect on $w_{ic}$ of the fact that the prices are $p_{1c}, \ldots, p_{nc}$ rather than $\bar{p}_1, \ldots, \bar{p}_n$.

For this purpose we take the total differential of $w_i = p_i q_i / M$:

$$dw_i = w_i \, d(\log p_i) + w_i \, d(\log q_i) - w_i \, d(\log M)$$

We write this in a slightly different form,

$$\begin{aligned} dw_i = {} & w_i[d(\log p_i) - d(\log P)] + w_i \, d(\log q_i) \\ & - w_i[d(\log M) - d(\log P)] \end{aligned} \qquad \text{(C9)}$$

where d(log $P$) is the Divisia price index. The expression in brackets in the second line vanishes because real income is fixed at the level $Q_c$ (see the second paragraph of Section 5). Thus, (C9) is simplified to

$$dw_i = w_i[d(\log p_i) - d(\log P)] + w_i \, d(\log q_i) \qquad \text{(C10)}$$

The expression on the far right is the dependent variable of the differential demand equation (C7). The real-income term in (C7) vanishes, so that (C10) can be expressed in terms of price changes only:

$$dw_i = w_i[d(\log p_i) - d(\log P)] + \phi\theta_i[d(\log p_i) - d(\log P^*)] \qquad \text{(C11)}$$

The price terms (5.6) and (5.7) are then immediately obtained by interpreting d(log $p_i$) as $\log p_{ic} - \log \bar{p}_i$ and applying the mean value theorem of differential calculus as well as (5.2) and (5.3) for the budget and marginal shares $w_i$ and $\theta_i$, respectively.

## APPENDIX D

### The estimation procedure

The ML procedure is described in Section 2.10 of Theil et al. (1989). When $\Omega$ is known, ML amounts to nonlinear generalized least squares. For MI we need the derivatives of $\bar{I}$ [cf. (2.2)] with respect to $w_{ic}$ for $i = 1, \ldots, n-1$. This derivative takes the form

$$-(1/N) \sum_{c=1}^{N} \log(w_{ic}/\hat{w}_{ic} - w_{nc}/\hat{w}_{nc})$$

where $\hat{w}_{nc}$ equals one minus the sum of $\hat{w}_{jc}$ over $j = 1, \ldots, n-1$. The derivative of $\bar{I}$ with respect to the parameter vector can then be obtained by means of the chain rule. We used the OPTMUM procedure in GAUSS for the minimization of $\bar{I}$.

For the true values of the coefficients and $\Omega$ in the simulation experiment of Table 4-4 see Tables D-3 and 3-4 (lower part) of Theil et al. (1989). The corresponding experiment of Table 4-6 is based on the coefficient values in the second-last column of Table 1 of Seale et al. (1991) and on the $\Omega$ shown below (multiplied by $10^6$). The numbering of the rows corresponds to that column 1 of Table 4-5.

$$\begin{bmatrix}
1629 & -120 & 57 & -224 & -147 & -155 & -206 & -284 & -169 & -126 \\
 & 496 & -12 & -143 & -32 & 8 & -32 & -0 & 48 & -3 \\
 & & 266 & -84 & -80 & 74 & -18 & -159 & -49 & 11 \\
 & & & 475 & 47 & -71 & 8 & 38 & -33 & 3 \\
 & & & & 260 & -30 & -4 & 15 & -18 & 24 \\
 & & & & & 287 & -30 & -50 & 12 & -11 \\
 & & & & & & 270 & -5 & 26 & -60 \\
 & & & & & & & 486 & 30 & -37 \\
 & & & & & & & & 176 & -16 \\
 & & & & & & & & & 256
\end{bmatrix}
\begin{matrix} 1 \\ 2 \\ 3 \\ 4 \\ 5 \\ 6 \\ 7 \\ 8 \\ 9 \\ 10 \end{matrix}$$

## References

Finke, R., Flood, L.R. and Theil, H. (1984). "Minimum information estimation of allocation models of different sizes." *Statistics and Probability Letters* 2: 279–282.

Finke, R. and Theil, H. (1984). "An extended version of minimum information estimation of allocation models." *Economics Letters* 15: 229–233.

Flood, L.R., Finke, R. and Theil, H. (1984). "Maximum likelihood and minimum information estimation of allocation models with fat-tailed error distributions." *Economics Letters* 16: 213–218.

Geary, R.C. (1958). "A note on the comparison of exchange rates and purchasing power between countries." *Journal of the Royal Statistical Society*, Series A, 121: 97–99.

Khamis, S.H. (1967). "Some problems relating to the international comparability and fluctuations of production volume indicators." *Bulletin of the International Statistical Institute* 42, Part 1: 213–230.

Khamis, S.H. (1970). "Properties and conditions for the existence of a new type of index numbers." *Sankhyā*, Series B, 32: 81–98.

Khamis, S.H. (1972). "A new system of index numbers for national and international purposes." *Journal of the Royal Statistical Society*, Series A, 135: 96–121.

Kravis, I.B., Heston, A.W. and Summers, R. (1978). *International Comparisons of Real Product and Purchasing Power*. Baltimore, Md.: The Johns Hopkins University Press.

Kravis, I.B., Heston, A.W. and Summers, R. (1982). *World Product and Income: International Comparison of Real Gross Product*. Baltimore, Md.: The Johns Hopkins University Press.

Kravis, I.B., Kenessey, Z., Heston, A.W. and Summers, R. (1975). *A System of International Comparisons of Gross Product and Purchasing Power*. Baltimore, Md.: The Johns Hopkins University Press.

Laitinen, K. (1978). "Why is demand homogeneity so often rejected?" *Economics Letters* 1: 187–191. Also in Raj and Koerts (1992), Ch. 29.

Meisner, J.F. (1979). "The sad fate of the asymptotic Slutsky symmetry test for large systems." *Economics Letters* 2: 231–233. Also in Raj and Koerts (1992), Ch. 30.

Raj, B. and Koerts, J. (1992). *Henri Theil's Contributions to Economics and Econometrics*. Three volumes. Dordrecht/Boston/London: Kluwer Academic Publishers.

Seale, J.L., Jr., Walker, W.E. and Kim, I.-M. (1991). "The demand for energy: Cross-country evidence using the Florida model." *Energy Economics* 13: 33–39.

Shannon, C.E. (1948). "A mathematical theory of communication." *Bell System Technical Journal* 27: 379–423, 623–656.

Strobel, D. (1982). "Determining outliers in multivariate surveys by decomposition of a measure of information." *Proceedings of the American Statistical Association, Business and Economic Statistics Section*, 31–35. Washington, D.C.: American Statistical Association.

Theil, H. (1975). *Theory and Measurement of Consumer Demand*, Volume 1. Amsterdam: North-Holland Publishing Company.

Theil, H., Chung, C.-F. and Seale, J.L., Jr. (1989). *International Evidence on Consumption Patterns*. Greenwich, Conn.: JAI Press Inc.

Theil, H. and Clements, K.W. (1987). *Applied Demand Analysis: Results from System-Wide Approaches*. Cambridge, Mass.: Ballinger Publishing Company.

Theil, H., Finke, R. and Flood, L.R. (1984). "Minimum information estimation of allocation models." *Economics Letters* 15: 251–256.

Working, H. (1943). "Statistical laws of family expenditure." *Journal of the American Statistical Association* 38: 43–56.

CHAPTER 5

# Cross-country variation of real income and relative prices

HENRI THEIL and DONGLING CHEN

**Abstract.** PPP – based data (PPP = purchasing power parity) from the International Comparison Project are used to analyze per capita real incomes and relative prices of 30 countries. One result is a cross-country covariance matrix of real income and relative prices; it indicates that food becomes relatively less expensive when we move from poor to richer countries. A second result is a matrix showing distances of relative price vectors for pairs of countries. A third result is a pair of price variances associated with the Florida model for cross-country demand analysis.

## 1. Some dimensional considerations

In this chapter we shall be interested in the cross-country variation of income and prices. Let $p_{1c}, \ldots, p_{nc}$ be the prices of $n$ goods in country $c$, and let $Q_c$ be its per capita real income. The data matrix in (natural) logarithms for $N$ countries will then take the following form:

$$\begin{bmatrix} \log p_{11} & \ldots & \log p_{n1} & \log Q_1 \\ \cdot & & \cdot & \cdot \\ \cdot & & \cdot & \cdot \\ \cdot & & \cdot & \cdot \\ \log p_{1N} & \ldots & \log p_{nN} & \log Q_N \end{bmatrix} \begin{matrix} \text{country } 1 \\ \\ \\ \\ \text{country } N \end{matrix} \tag{1.1}$$

To fit a cross-country demand model we need adequate variation in income and prices across countries. How can we measure such a dispersion across countries? The answer for the last column of the matrix (1.1), dealing with per capita real income, is straightforward. We write $q_c = \log Q_c$ and consider its variance across countries,

$$\frac{1}{N} \sum_{c=1}^{N} (q_c - \bar{q})^2 \tag{1.2}$$

where $\bar{q}$ is the arithmetic mean of $q_c$ over $c$. However, the extension of (1.2) to any other column of (1.1),

$$\frac{1}{N} \sum_{c=1}^{N} \left( \log p_{ic} - \frac{1}{N} \sum_{d=1}^{N} \log p_{id} \right)^2 \tag{1.3}$$

would be unacceptable. To understand this we must recognize that the International Comparison Project computes prices by dividing expenditures in national currency by expenditures in international prices. This means that the prices $p_{1c}, \ldots, p_{nc}$ of all goods in country c have the same dimension, but that $p_{ic}$ and $p_{id}$ have different dimensions for different countries $c$ and $d$. We can raise French prices artificially by expressing them in centimes rather than francs. This would raise each log $p_{ic}$ by log 100 for $c$ = France, this allowing France to dominate the variance (1.3), but this would be entirely arbitrary.

To solve this problem we should recognize that our interest must be in relative rather than absolute prices (in the same way that what really counts is real income, not money income). Let $\bar{w}_k$ be the arithmetic mean of the budget shares $w_{k1}, \ldots, w_{kN}$ of good $k$ in the $N$ countries. Following Theil and Fiebig (1986), we deflate each price $p_{ic}$ by the weighted geometric mean of $p_{1c}, \ldots, p_{nc}$ (same country $c$!) with weights $\bar{w}_1, \ldots, \bar{w}_n$. In logarithmic terms:

$$z_{ic} = \log p_{ic} - \sum_{k=1}^{N} \bar{w}_k \log p_{kc} \tag{1.4}$$

The problem raised at the end of the previous paragraph does not occur when log $p_{ic}$ is replaced by $z_{ic}$, because multiplying all pries $p_{1c}, \ldots, p_{nc}$ of country $c$ by any positive number $k$ leaves $z_{ic}$ unchanged.

## 2. The dispersion of real income and relative prices

The results just obtained suggests that we should replace the data matrix (1.1) by

$$\begin{bmatrix} z_{11} & \cdots & z_{n1} & q_1 \\ \cdot & & \cdot & \cdot \\ \cdot & & \cdot & \cdot \\ \cdot & & \cdot & \cdot \\ z_{1N} & \cdots & z_{nN} & q_N \end{bmatrix} \begin{matrix} \text{country 1} \\ \\ \\ \\ \text{country } N \end{matrix} \tag{2.1}$$

The last column is identical to that of the matrix (1.1), so that the variance (1.2) of real income per capita still applies. However, instead of (1.3) we now have

$$\frac{1}{N} \sum_{c=1}^{N} (z_{ic} - \bar{z}_i)^2 \tag{2.2}$$

which is the variance of the logarithmic *relative* prices of good $i$ across countries, with $\bar{z}_i$ defined as

$$\bar{z}_i = \log \bar{p}_i - \sum_{k=1}^{n} \bar{w}_k \log \bar{p}_k \tag{2.3}$$

where $\overline{p}_i$ is the geometric mean of the prices of good $i$ in the $N$ countries:

$$\log \overline{p}_i = \frac{1}{N} \sum_{c=1}^{N} \log p_{ic} \tag{2.4}$$

We conclude from (1.4) and (2.3) that the expression in parentheses in (2.2) can be written as

$$z_{ic} - \overline{z}_i = \log \frac{p_{ic}}{\overline{p}_i} - \sum_{k=1}^{n} \overline{w}_k \log \frac{p_{kc}}{\overline{p}_k} \tag{2.5}$$

Note that the logarithms on the right have the same form as those which occur in the two price terms of the Florida model.

The variances (1.2) and (2.2) are the diagonal elements of the matrix shown in Table 5-1. This matrix is based on the 1975 data for $N = 30$ countries for $n = 10$ consumption goods: (1) Food; (2) Beverages and tobacco; (3) Clothing and footwear; (4) Gross rent and fuel; (5) House furnishings and operations; (6) Medical care; (7) Transport and communications; (8) Recreation; (9) Education; (10) Other consumption expenditures. The names of these goods are also shown (in abbreviated form) in the second top row of the table.

The off-diagonal elements of the matrix in this table are the covariances associated with the variances (1.2) and (2.2). Those in the last column of the table are of the form

$$\frac{1}{N} \sum_{c=1}^{N} (q_c - \overline{q})(z_{ic} - \overline{z}_i) \tag{2.6}$$

*Table 5-1.* The covariance matrix of the logs of relative prices and real income in 1975

| Relative price of | | | | | | | | | | Real |
|---|---|---|---|---|---|---|---|---|---|---|
| Food | Beverages | Clothing | Rent | House | Medical | Transport | Recreation | Education | Other | income |
| (1) | (2) | (3) | (4) | (5) | (6) | (7) | (8) | (9) | (10) | (11) |
| 266 | 144 | –21 | –117 | –25 | –190 | –83 | –61 | –644 | –131 | –847 |
| | 1038 | 226 | –256 | 78 | –718 | 307 | –202 | –806 | –207 | –975 |
| | | 396 | –203 | 153 | –386 | 176 | –46 | –221 | –26 | 42 |
| | | | 738 | –123 | 385 | –405 | –107 | 203 | –38 | 102 |
| | | | | 468 | –154 | 184 | 148 | –543 | –100 | –327 |
| | | | | | 1165 | –414 | 229 | 547 | 159 | 459 |
| | | | | | | 575 | 47 | 11 | 4 | 289 |
| | | | | | | | 449 | –226 | 90 | –244 |
| | | | | | | | | 3421 | 504 | 3806 |
| | | | | | | | | | 217 | 555 |
| | | | | | | | | | | 5118 |

*Note:* All entries to be multiplied by $10^{-4}$.
*Source:* Theil et al. (1989), Table 2-1.

Such a covariance measures the co-movement of per capita real income and a relative price across countries. The covariance in all other columns take the form

$$\frac{1}{N} \sum_{c=1}^{N} (z_{ic} - \bar{z}_i)(z_{jc} - \bar{z}_j) \tag{2.7}$$

which measures the co-movement of the relative prices of two goods across countries.

The 11 diagonal elements in Table 5-1 show that the variance (1.2) exceeds that in (2.2) for each $i$. Thus, there is more cross-country dispersion of real income than of any of the relative prices. Of all 10 prices, Education has by far the largest relative price dispersion across countries. A major cause is the large role of teachers' salaries in educational expenditures, since these salaries are highly correlated with per capita income across countries. Indeed, by taking the three appropriate entries in Table 5-1, we find that the cross-country correlation coefficient of $q_c$ and $z_{9c}$ ($i = 9$ is Education) equals 0.91. Also note that the analogous correlation for Food ($i = 1$) equals – 0.73. This means that Food becomes relative inexpensive (relative to other goods and services) when we move from poor to more affluent countries.

## 3. Distances between vectors of relative prices

In the previous section we concentrated our attention on the columns of the matrix (2.1), but it is also instructive to consider this matrix row by row, particularly for the submatrix that deals with prices. We reproduce this matrix here:

$$\begin{bmatrix} z_{11} & z_{21} & \cdots & z_{n1} \\ \cdot & \cdot & & \cdot \\ \cdot & \cdot & & \cdot \\ \cdot & \cdot & & \cdot \\ z_{1N} & z_{2N} & \cdots & z_{nN} \end{bmatrix} \begin{matrix} \text{country } 1 \\ \\ \\ \\ \text{country } N \end{matrix} \tag{3.1}$$

It follows directly from (1.4) that, for each country $c$, the weighted mean (with weights $\bar{w}_1, \ldots, \bar{w}_N$) of the $z_{ic}$'s vanishes:

$$\sum_{i=1}^{n} \bar{w}_i z_{ic} = 0 \tag{3.2}$$

Next consider the variances and covariances associated with this weighted mean:

$$\sum_{i=1}^{n} \bar{w}_i z_{ic}^2 \quad \text{and} \quad \sum_{i=1}^{n} \bar{w}_i z_{ic} z_{id} \tag{3.3}$$

Recall that the variance (2.2) is the variance of the relative prices of one good across countries, and that the covariance (2.7) is the covariance of the relative prices of the two goods ($i$ and $j$) across countries. By contrast, the variance shown in (3.3) is a (weighted) variance of relative prices across goods in one country. Similarly, the covariance in (3.3) is a (weighted) covariance of the relative prices across goods in two countries ($c$ and $d$).

We can use these new variances and covariances to define distances between vectors of relative prices in the $n$-dimensional logarithmic price space. We represent each country $c$ by a price point $P_c$ whose $i^{\text{th}}$ coordinate is $S_i z_{ic}$, where $S_i$ is the positive square root of $\bar{w}_i$. The variance shown in (3.3) is then equal to $(OP_c)^2$; that is, the squared distance between the origin ($O$) and $P_c$. Similarly, the squared distance between the price points of countries $c$ and $d$ takes the form

$$(P_c P_d)^2 = \sum_{i=1}^{n} \bar{w}_i (z_{ic}^2 + z_{id}^2 - 2 z_{ic} z_{id}) \tag{3.4}$$

On comparing this expression with the variance and covariance shown in (3.3), we conclude that the squared distance between the price points of $c$ and $d$ equals the sum of two variances minus twice the covariance.

The upper right part of Table 5-2, from Theil and Seale (1987), shows the distance $P_c P_d$ (not squared!), multiplied by 1000, for the $n = 10$ goods and $N = 30$ countries in 1975. The countries are listed in the table in the order of declining per capita income ($Q_1 \geq Q_2 \geq \ldots \geq Q_{30}$). Note that the distances between the industrially advanced countries (the first 12) are all below 0.4. The distances between any of these countries and any of the four Communist countries (13, 16, 18, 19) and any of the underdeveloped countries tend to be much larger.

Recall from the last paragraph of Section 2 that the relative price of Education is highly correlated with per capita real income. This suggests that Education should be a major contributor to the price distances between rich and poor countries. To verify this was delete Education (good 9) from the 10 goods by replacing $\bar{w}_i$ by the arithmetic average (over $c = 1, \ldots, 30$) of $w_{ic}/(1 - w_{9c})$ for each i $\neq$ 9. This results, shown below the diagonal in Table 5-2, corroborate that deleting Education yields substantially smaller price distances between the rich and the poor. For example, there are nine distances between each of the three richest countries and each of the three poorest. These nine distances are between 0.54 and 0.69 in the upper right corner of Table 5-2, whereas they are between 0.31 and 0.52 in the lower left part.

*Table 5-2.* Distances in 1975 between the relative price vectors of 30 countries for 10 goods (above diagonal) and 9 goods (below diagonal)

| | | (1) | (2) | (3) | (4) | (5) | (6) | (7) | (8) | (9) | (10) | (11) | (12) | (13) | (14) | (15) |
|---|---|---|---|---|---|---|---|---|---|---|---|---|---|---|---|---|
| 1 | Unites States | 0 | 225 | 282 | 178 | 129 | 230 | 169 | 128 | 337 | 323 | 229 | 215 | 462 | 304 | 452 |
| 2 | Luxembourg | 224 | 0 | 200 | 141 | 188 | 250 | 104 | 215 | 242 | 328 | 201 | 189 | 364 | 289 | 457 |
| 3 | Denmark | 292 | 199 | 0 | 185 | 175 | 194 | 188 | 218 | 165 | 345 | 219 | 181 | 312 | 204 | 421 |
| 4 | France | 178 | 98 | 183 | 0 | 110 | 160 | 78 | 152 | 252 | 252 | 188 | 129 | 346 | 245 | 381 |
| 5 | Germany | 127 | 165 | 175 | 114 | 0 | 144 | 125 | 116 | 237 | 281 | 177 | 142 | 364 | 203 | 394 |
| 6 | Austria | 219 | 207 | 174 | 158 | 139 | 0 | 206 | 196 | 266 | 195 | 228 | 140 | 323 | 227 | 318 |
| 7 | Belgium | 175 | 91 | 194 | 64 | 122 | 190 | 0 | 154 | 230 | 295 | 174 | 158 | 366 | 245 | 406 |
| 8 | Netherlands | 128 | 220 | 224 | 136 | 96 | 160 | 156 | 0 | 307 | 341 | 259 | 227 | 454 | 281 | 456 |
| 9 | United Kingdom | 348 | 236 | 168 | 259 | 244 | 266 | 236 | 313 | 0 | 359 | 232 | 239 | 248 | 126 | 375 |
| 10 | Spain | 263 | 208 | 285 | 205 | 237 | 166 | 221 | 259 | 322 | 0 | 281 | 215 | 301 | 320 | 228 |
| 11 | Japan | 222 | 150 | 208 | 191 | 178 | 236 | 158 | 242 | 232 | 262 | 0 | 127 | 315 | 253 | 398 |
| 12 | Italy | 201 | 116 | 156 | 124 | 135 | 145 | 130 | 196 | 236 | 192 | 131 | 0 | 288 | 239 | 345 |
| 13 | Hungary | 434 | 272 | 248 | 323 | 341 | 317 | 319 | 409 | 186 | 311 | 303 | 279 | 0 | 262 | 296 |
| 14 | Ireland | 301 | 257 | 187 | 249 | 203 | 235 | 235 | 263 | 112 | 309 | 261 | 246 | 247 | 0 | 318 |
| 15 | Uruguay | 371 | 322 | 323 | 313 | 326 | 267 | 306 | 350 | 286 | 222 | 358 | 303 | 294 | 265 | 0 |
| 16 | Poland | 486 | 381 | 265 | 390 | 390 | 339 | 408 | 438 | 294 | 388 | 403 | 338 | 210 | 313 | 360 |
| 17 | Mexico | 229 | 251 | 303 | 200 | 241 | 216 | 236 | 217 | 422 | 239 | 291 | 204 | 451 | 410 | 394 |
| 18 | Yugoslavia | 340 | 245 | 177 | 254 | 257 | 191 | 271 | 302 | 238 | 221 | 254 | 190 | 190 | 251 | 270 |
| 19 | Romania | 622 | 539 | 417 | 528 | 538 | 439 | 556 | 555 | 481 | 476 | 557 | 480 | 398 | 492 | 446 |
| 20 | Iran | 182 | 294 | 318 | 271 | 210 | 221 | 276 | 245 | 375 | 267 | 266 | 213 | 436 | 336 | 364 |
| 21 | Syria | 250 | 166 | 169 | 180 | 178 | 148 | 182 | 242 | 197 | 165 | 187 | 107 | 212 | 199 | 219 |
| 22 | Colombia | 135 | 224 | 258 | 193 | 149 | 161 | 207 | 178 | 338 | 214 | 212 | 144 | 391 | 307 | 342 |
| 23 | Brazil | 269 | 194 | 216 | 186 | 203 | 201 | 163 | 245 | 182 | 214 | 238 | 194 | 269 | 177 | 174 |
| 24 | Korea | 328 | 283 | 335 | 332 | 308 | 319 | 336 | 376 | 377 | 315 | 235 | 241 | 354 | 392 | 459 |
| 25 | Malaysia | 318 | 267 | 199 | 281 | 225 | 202 | 287 | 302 | 209 | 278 | 240 | 211 | 245 | 200 | 328 |
| 26 | Thailand | 194 | 237 | 231 | 201 | 165 | 166 | 191 | 192 | 286 | 239 | 211 | 161 | 384 | 268 | 294 |
| 27 | Philippines | 377 | 275 | 258 | 316 | 316 | 289 | 325 | 383 | 323 | 318 | 252 | 203 | 290 | 366 | 412 |
| 28 | Sri Lanka | 524 | 430 | 344 | 456 | 436 | 414 | 480 | 500 | 404 | 483 | 428 | 384 | 344 | 428 | 549 |
| 29 | Pakistan | 316 | 308 | 432 | 361 | 345 | 446 | 332 | 407 | 418 | 436 | 278 | 337 | 462 | 426 | 537 |
| 30 | India | 434 | 342 | 318 | 374 | 377 | 371 | 385 | 439 | 338 | 383 | 366 | 306 | 256 | 354 | 398 |

| | | (16) | (17) | (18) | (19) | (20) | (21) | (22) | (23) | (24) | (25) | (26) | (27) | (28) | (29) | (30) |
|---|---|---|---|---|---|---|---|---|---|---|---|---|---|---|---|---|
| 1 | Unites States | 521 | 268 | 380 | 652 | 241 | 372 | 261 | 457 | 418 | 369 | 322 | 514 | 690 | 543 | 642 |
| 2 | Luxembourg | 465 | 321 | 344 | 608 | 363 | 378 | 359 | 474 | 430 | 368 | 395 | 499 | 673 | 589 | 638 |
| 3 | Denmark | 347 | 333 | 262 | 480 | 353 | 333 | 342 | 437 | 429 | 286 | 350 | 446 | 581 | 619 | 581 |
| 4 | France | 418 | 221 | 286 | 552 | 289 | 295 | 261 | 377 | 394 | 316 | 292 | 441 | 613 | 535 | 571 |
| 5 | Germany | 421 | 259 | 292 | 562 | 240 | 299 | 237 | 390 | 379 | 273 | 275 | 445 | 603 | 529 | 577 |
| 6 | Austria | 356 | 218 | 211 | 455 | 227 | 240 | 208 | 346 | 359 | 226 | 235 | 391 | 552 | 562 | 535 |
| 7 | Belgium | 456 | 275 | 326 | 595 | 316 | 336 | 305 | 411 | 426 | 346 | 324 | 483 | 663 | 555 | 615 |
| 8 | Netherlands | 496 | 278 | 367 | 608 | 308 | 391 | 310 | 471 | 474 | 375 | 347 | 540 | 696 | 621 | 669 |
| 9 | United Kingdom | 350 | 428 | 286 | 519 | 390 | 323 | 386 | 395 | 443 | 272 | 366 | 462 | 594 | 588 | 567 |
| 10 | Spain | 377 | 237 | 214 | 464 | 260 | 180 | 209 | 271 | 313 | 269 | 239 | 348 | 539 | 490 | 468 |
| 11 | Japan | 416 | 290 | 270 | 566 | 272 | 272 | 253 | 376 | 299 | 264 | 274 | 374 | 569 | 457 | 539 |
| 12 | Italy | 353 | 205 | 208 | 491 | 218 | 217 | 193 | 340 | 294 | 232 | 230 | 334 | 529 | 483 | 492 |
| 13 | Hungary | 206 | 439 | 184 | 390 | 423 | 224 | 380 | 319 | 352 | 238 | 378 | 328 | 433 | 516 | 384 |
| 14 | Ireland | 334 | 402 | 264 | 504 | 335 | 275 | 328 | 336 | 423 | 226 | 313 | 449 | 564 | 549 | 526 |
| 15 | Uruguay | 352 | 401 | 274 | 432 | 369 | 213 | 335 | 196 | 445 | 325 | 285 | 409 | 566 | 548 | 440 |
| 16 | Poland | 0 | 456 | 188 | 236 | 448 | 273 | 404 | 384 | 403 | 280 | 414 | 327 | 357 | 598 | 333 |
| 17 | Mexico | 465 | 0 | 310 | 528 | 244 | 295 | 190 | 386 | 361 | 369 | 252 | 382 | 584 | 524 | 536 |
| 18 | Yugoslavia | 191 | 317 | 0 | 312 | 315 | 159 | 262 | 310 | 289 | 188 | 288 | 276 | 413 | 518 | 382 |
| 19 | Romania | 243 | 536 | 316 | 0 | 564 | 413 | 518 | 505 | 539 | 435 | 519 | 440 | 460 | 768 | 460 |
| 20 | Iran | 459 | 252 | 325 | 576 | 0 | 256 | 110 | 358 | 294 | 267 | 187 | 355 | 550 | 457 | 501 |
| 21 | Syria | 275 | 272 | 133 | 425 | 235 | 0 | 190 | 178 | 256 | 186 | 188 | 227 | 407 | 402 | 325 |
| 22 | Colombia | 418 | 180 | 268 | 535 | 95 | 188 | 0 | 297 | 251 | 246 | 149 | 299 | 492 | 407 | 440 |
| 23 | Brazil | 365 | 323 | 257 | 506 | 299 | 157 | 265 | 0 | 397 | 310 | 218 | 337 | 493 | 415 | 381 |
| 24 | Korea | 414 | 351 | 287 | 557 | 283 | 264 | 254 | 395 | 0 | 257 | 334 | 211 | 380 | 341 | 380 |
| 25 | Malaysia | 289 | 377 | 194 | 447 | 273 | 174 | 254 | 266 | 255 | 0 | 260 | 281 | 395 | 470 | 416 |
| 26 | Thailand | 426 | 233 | 288 | 536 | 166 | 193 | 150 | 192 | 344 | 262 | 0 | 313 | 520 | 437 | 462 |
| 27 | Philippines | 307 | 328 | 224 | 441 | 306 | 220 | 275 | 347 | 197 | 239 | 306 | 0 | 279 | 399 | 273 |
| 28 | Sri Lanka | 270 | 506 | 315 | 419 | 474 | 374 | 442 | 499 | 336 | 302 | 493 | 266 | 0 | 518 | 271 |
| 29 | Pakistan | 573 | 446 | 465 | 768 | 371 | 379 | 352 | 422 | 301 | 414 | 409 | 403 | 535 | 0 | 427 |
| 30 | India | 215 | 432 | 250 | 410 | 398 | 262 | 367 | 377 | 325 | 316 | 417 | 251 | 279 | 440 | 0 |

*Note:* All entries are to be multiplied by $10^{-3}$. *Source:* Theil and Seale (1987).

## 4. The Divisia and Frisch price variances of the Florida model

In the previous sections we used $\overline{w}_i$, the arithmetic mean of $w_{i1}, \ldots, w_{iN}$, as the weight of the deflator used to obtain relative prices. There are other possible deflators. We recall that the Florida model takes the following form:

$$w_{ic} = \alpha_i + \beta_i q_c + (\alpha_i + \beta_i q_c)\left[\log\frac{p_{ic}}{\overline{p}_i} - \sum_{j=1}^{n}(\alpha_j + \beta_j q_c)\log\frac{p_{jc}}{\overline{p}_j}\right]$$
$$+ \phi(\alpha_i + \beta_i q_c^*)\left[\log\frac{p_{ic}}{\overline{p}_i} - \sum_{j=1}^{n}(\alpha_j + \beta_j q_c^*)\log\frac{p_{jc}}{\overline{p}_j}\right] + \varepsilon_{ic}$$

Here $\alpha_i + \beta_i q_c$ and $\alpha_i + \beta_i q_c^*$ are the budget and marginal share, respectively, of good $i$ at geometric mean prices and the per capita real income of country $c$.

We multiply both sides of the equation by $\log(p_{ic}/\overline{p}_i)$ and then sum over $i = 1, \ldots, n$. It is easily seen that, after minor rearrangements, the result can be written as

$$\sum_{i=1}^{n} w_{ic}\log\frac{p_{ic}}{\overline{p}_i} = \sum_{i=1}^{n}(\alpha_i + \beta_i q_c)\log\frac{p_{ic}}{\overline{p}_i} + \Pi_c + \phi\Pi_c^* + \text{error} \qquad (4.1)$$

where $\Pi_c$ and $\Pi_c^*$ are two variances of logarithmic price changes:

$$\Pi_c = \sum_{i=1}^{n}(\alpha_i + \beta_i q_c)\left[\log\frac{p_{ic}}{\overline{p}_i} - \sum_{j=1}^{n}(\alpha_j + \beta_j q_c)\log\frac{p_{jc}}{\overline{p}_j}\right]^2 \qquad (4.2)$$

$$\Pi_c^* = \sum_{i=1}^{n}(\alpha_i + \beta_i q_c^*)\left[\log\frac{p_{ic}}{\overline{p}_i} - \sum_{j=1}^{n}(\alpha_j + \beta_j q_c^*)\log\frac{p_{jc}}{\overline{p}_j}\right]^2 \qquad (4.3)$$

Given the interpretation of $\alpha_i + \beta_i q_c$ and $\alpha_i + \beta_i q_c^*$ as budget and marginal shares, respectively, we shall refer to $\Pi_c$ as the Divisia variance and to $\Pi_c^*$ as the Frisch variance of country $c$.[1] Both variances measure the degree of disproportionality of the $n$ price changes from $(\overline{p}_1, \ldots, \overline{p}_n)$ to $(p_{1c}, \ldots, p_{nc})$, but they employ different weights.

The computation of these two variances requires a numerical specification of the $\alpha$'s and $\beta$'s. When we select those given in Table 4-4 (column 2) of Chapter 4, we obtain the price variances shown in columns 2 and 3 of Table 5-3. The Frisch variance exceeds the Divisia variance in most cases. There are four countries for which both variances exceeds 0.1: the three poorest (India, Pakistan and Sri Lanka) and communist Romania. The two variances of all 26 other countries are smaller than 0.1. This difference reflects the larger degree of disproportionality in the change from geometric mean prices to the observed prices of the four countries mentioned.

[1] Divisia variances and covariances use budget shares as weights, whereas their Frisch counterparts use marginal shares instead.

*Table 5-3.* Divisia and Frisch price variances of the Florida model, 1975

| Country (1) | | $\Pi_c$ (2) | $\Pi_c^*$ (3) | $\phi$ (4) |
|---|---|---|---|---|
| 1 | USA | 0.0586 | 0.0701 | –1.17 |
| 2 | Luxembourg | 0.0704 | 0.0746 | –1.18 |
| 3 | Denmark | 0.0455 | 0.0503 | –1.27 |
| 4 | France | 0.0369 | 0.0384 | –1.43 |
| 5 | Germany | 0.0338 | 0.0370 | –0.97 |
| 6 | Austria | 0.0211 | 0.0241 | 0.11 |
| 7 | Belgium | 0.0556 | 0.0564 | –1.49 |
| 8 | Netherlands | 0.0805 | 0.0858 | –1.11 |
| 9 | United Kingdom | 0.0603 | 0.0619 | –0.74 |
| 10 | Spain | 0.0312 | 0.0349 | –0.96 |
| 11 | Japan | 0.0326 | 0.0373 | –0.16 |
| 12 | Italy | 0.0120 | 0.0132 | –1.43 |
| 13 | Hungary | 0.0501 | 0.0618 | –0.83 |
| 14 | Ireland | 0.0444 | 0.0398 | –2.06 |
| 15 | Uruguay | 0.0753 | 0.0756 | –0.81 |
| 16 | Poland | 0.0816 | 0.0914 | –0.45 |
| 17 | Mexico | 0.0611 | 0.0705 | –0.51 |
| 18 | Yugoslavia | 0.0202 | 0.0243 | –0.29 |
| 19 | Romania | 0.2050 | 0.2445 | –0.89 |
| 20 | Iran | 0.0509 | 0.0598 | –0.56 |
| 21 | Syria | 0.0145 | 0.0158 | –0.43 |
| 22 | Colombia | 0.0299 | 0.0351 | –1.18 |
| 23 | Brazil | 0.0680 | 0.0656 | –1.27 |
| 24 | Korea | 0.0572 | 0.0384 | –1.57 |
| 25 | Malaysia | 0.0285 | 0.0321 | –1.13 |
| 26 | Thailand | 0.0408 | 0.0435 | –0.51 |
| 27 | Philippines | 0.0690 | 0.0564 | –1.43 |
| 28 | Sri Lanka | 0.1881 | 0.1547 | –1.68 |
| 29 | Pakistan | 0.2188 | 0.2449 | –0.86 |
| 30 | India | 0.1619 | 0.1529 | –1.63 |

## 5. Frisch's conjecture on the income flexibility

When we subtract the first two terms on the right in (4.1) from the expression on the left, we obtain

$$N_c = \sum_{j=1}^{n} (w_{ic} - \alpha_i + \beta_i q_c) \log \frac{p_{ic}}{\overline{p}_i} - \Pi_c \tag{5.1}$$

The equation thus states that $N_c$ equals $\phi\Pi_c^*$ plus an error term. Ignoring the error, we can regard the ratio $N_c/\Pi_c^*$ as an estimate of $\phi$ for country $c$. The estimates are shown in column 4 of Table 5-3. They are a bit volatile; about the best thing that can be said is that all except one have the correct (negative) sign.

Nevertheless, this exercise is of some importance because of a conjecture made by Ragnar Frisch (1959: 189). Frisch denies that $\phi$ is a constant. In fact, he provides explicit numerical statements on the dependence of $1/\phi$ (the income elasticity of the marginal utility of income) on the level of real income. We quote him below; the words in brackets are adaptions to the terminology used here.

"We may, perhaps, assume that in most cases the [income elasticity of the marginal utility of income] has values of the order of magnitude give below.

- 10 for an extremely poor and apathetic part of the population.
- 4 for the slightly better off but still poor part of the population with a fairly pronounced desire to become better off.
- 2 for the middle income bracket, 'the median part' of the population.
- 0.7 for the better off part of the population.
- 0.1 for the rich part of the population with ambitions toward 'conspicuous consumption.'

It would be a very promising research project to determine [the income elasticity of the marginal utility of income] for different countries and different types of populations. A universal 'atlas' of the values of [this elasticity] should be constructed. It would serve an extremely useful purpose in demand analysis."

One way of verifying Frisch's conjecture is by grouping the 30 countries of Table 5-3 by affluence: the top 10, the middle 10 and the bottom 10. We sum $N_c$ defined in (5.1) over the countries of each group and divide this sum by the corresponding sum of $\Pi_c^*$. This yields a $\phi$ estimate of –1.09 for the top 10, –0.77 for the middle 10 and –1.25 for the bottom 10. Evidently, these three numbers are not encouraging for the Frisch conjecture. We should be cautious, however, since the numbers in Table 5-3 are rather sensitive to the selected values of the $\alpha$'s and $\beta$'s.

## References


Frisch, R. (1959). "A complete scheme for computing all direct and cross demand elasticities in a model with many sectors." *Econometrica* 27: 177–196.

Theil, H., Chung, C.-F. and Seale, J.L., Jr. (1989). *International Evidence on Consumption Patterns*. Greenwich, Conn.: JAI Press Inc.

Theil, H. and Fiebig, D. (1986). "The measurement of income and price dispersion in cross-country demand systems." *Economics Letters* 22: 391–393.

Theil, H. and Seale, J.L., Jr. (1987). "Measuring the distance between relative price vectors of different countries." *Economics Letters* 23: 371–374.

CHAPTER 6

# The quality of consumption in rich and poor countries

HENRI THEIL and DONGLING CHEN

**Abstract.** We define the quality of the consumer's basket in terms of its luxury – necessity composition. The measure is applied to 30 countries in 1975, varying in affluence from the USA to India.

## 1. Measuring quality

It is appropriate to reflect on the question of whether the quality of consumption can be satisfactorily measured. Isn't quality an inherently subjective concept? Such questions have been raised before. For example, many physicists in the nineteenth century considered "warmth" too subjective to be measured. However, later on a general agreement emerged, and there are now two different useful ways of measuring this phenomenon: first, in the form of heat (measured in calories); second, in the form of temperature (measured along the Celsius or Kelvin scale).

Another example is the measurement of utility. This was taken for granted by many economists in the nineteenth and early twentieth century until the work of Hicks and Allen (1934) led to a more critical attitude. The later work by Von Neumann and Morgenstern (1947) convinced most economists that utility measurement is acceptable under conditions of uncertainty. Utility measurement under certainty is a different matter, but Frisch's (1959) ideas have numerous adherents, particularly among researchers of systems and subsystems of demand equations.

Here we adopt the view that there are at least three ways in which the quality of consumption can be measured. The most direct approach is based on an enumeration of the attractive features of a good, such as the horsepower and the size of an automobile. Unattractive features may also be included and should be counted negatively. This is the approach used in the theory of hedonic price indexes to explain price differentials of automobiles and of other goods. Such an approach is useful when we are interested in just one good at a time. However, it is less practical when dealing with several goods simultaneously. Indeed, this is the case here because we shall want to make a quality assessment based on the composition of total per capita consumption of each of a number of countries. It is then more attractive to summarize quality by means of a single number. How can this be done?

## 2. Luxuries versus necessities

One approach, suggested independently by Houthakker (1952) and Theil (1952), is based on the average price paid for a composite good (a non-homogenous good). Let coffee be such a good; it consists of several grades. Since high-quality coffee commands a higher price than low-quality coffee, one measure of the quality of the coffee bought by a household during a certain period is the average price which it paid for a pound of coffee (the total expenditure on coffee divided by the total quantity in pounds). Such an indicator is useful for a cross-section study when the prices of individual coffee grades are approximately constant during the short period covered by such a study. However, this method is applicable only to narrowly defined composite goods, since dimensional considerations prevent us from averaging the prices of coffee and (say) dental services. It is more attractive to measure quality by means of dimensionless concepts.

The distinction between luxuries and necessities based on income elasticities provides a solution. Let $p_i$ be the price of good $i$ and $q_i$ the quantity bought. Then $w_i = p_i q_i / M$ is the budget share of good $i$ and $\theta_i = \mathrm{d}(p_i q_i)/\mathrm{d}M$ its marginal share, where $M$ is total consumption expenditure. The ratio $\theta_i/w_i$ is the income elasticity of good $i$ (the elasticity with respect to total expenditure). Next consider the expression

$$\sum_{i=1}^{n} w_i \left( \frac{\theta_i}{w_i} - 1 \right) \mathrm{d}(\log q_i) \tag{2.1}$$

which is the Divisia covariance (the budget-share-weighted covariance) of the income elasticities and the logarithmic quantity changes. When the quantities consumed of luxuries increase relative to those of necessities, the covariance (2.1) is positive. The consumer reveals by his behavior that he considers luxuries more desirable than necessities, because he spends a larger fraction of his income on the former goods and a smaller fraction on the latter when he becomes more affluent (and when prices remain unchanged). Hence, a positive (negative) value of the covariance (2.1) indicates that the consumer's basket has increased (decreased) in desirability. Accordingly, we shall refer to the covariance (2.1) as the *quality index* of the consumer's basket in differential form.

The approaches of the two previous paragraphs, based respectively on the average price paid for a composite good and on the income elasticities of all $n$ goods, are both behavioral in the sense that they do not involve an outside judgement on what is "good" for the consumer. This is in contrast to the approach implicit in the hedonic price index theory, which may be viewed as claiming that "a powerful big car is good for you." Also, the former two approaches may be presumed to yield results that are positively correlated with each other. This may be illustrated with income elasticities (quoted from Cramer, 1973) obtained from a European household survey in 1963–1964. In Germany, where beer is cheap relative to wine, the income elasticity of beer is only 0.5 and that of wine is 1.3, but in Italy (where beer is expensive relative to wine) the income elasticity of beer is 1.1 and that of wine is only 0.7.

## 3. An application to 30 countries in 1975

Working's model has the property that the marginal share of each good $i$ exceeds its budget share by the (positive or negative) constant $\beta_i$, so that the covariance (2.1) becomes the sum of $\beta_i$ d(log $q_i$) over $i$. It is readily seen that the quality index in level (rather than differential) form can then be written as the product of $q_i^{\beta_i}$ over $i$. Thus, if we have data for each of 30 countries ($c = 1, \ldots, 30$) and if we want a quality index with base 1 for the United States ($c = 1$), the index in level form for country $c$ is

$$U_c = \sum_{i=1}^{n} (q_{ic}/q_{1i})^{\beta_i} \tag{3.1}$$

Here $q_{ic}$ is the 1975 volume of per capita expenditure of good $i$ in country $c$ (expressed in international prices as shown in columns 2 to 11 of Table 1-6 of Theil et al. [1989: 13–14] for $n = 10$ goods). When we specify $\beta_i$ as shown in column 2 of Table 4-4 of Chapter 4, we obtain the quality index values displayed in column 3 of Table 6-1. For comparison we show the volume index in column 2, taken from Theil et al. (1989: Table 1-6). The quality range is obviously much smaller than the quantity range.

We can express the covariance (2.1) as the sum of three components: real income, substitution and residual. This matter is pursued in the Appendix. It seems obvious that the real-income component should be dominant, which is confirmed by column 4 of Table 6-1.

*Table 6-1.* Quantity and quality indexes of consumption, 1975

| Country (1) | | Quantity index (2) | Quality index (3) | Real-income component of quality (4) |
|---|---|---|---|---|
| 1 | USA | 1.000 | 1.000 | 1.000 |
| 2 | Luxembourg | 0.794 | 0.949 | 0.965 |
| 3 | Denmark | 0.785 | 0.960 | 0.960 |
| 4 | France | 0.756 | 0.943 | 0.958 |
| 5 | Germany | 0.756 | 0.970 | 0.954 |
| 6 | Austria | 0.751 | 0.952 | 0.955 |
| 7 | Belgium | 0.750 | 0.930 | 0.957 |
| 8 | Netherlands | 0.686 | 0.936 | 0.941 |
| 9 | UK | 0.641 | 0.952 | 0.930 |
| 10 | Spain | 0.606 | 0.864 | 0.940 |
| 11 | Japan | 0.588 | 0.926 | 0.928 |
| 12 | Italy | 0.532 | 0.878 | 0.924 |
| 13 | Hungary | 0.467 | 0.888 | 0.904 |
| 14 | Ireland | 0.464 | 0.885 | 0.898 |
| 15 | Uruguay | 0.451 | 0.811 | 0.908 |
| 16 | Poland | 0.435 | 0.874 | 0.898 |
| 17 | Mexico | 0.371 | 0.827 | 0.894 |
| 18 | Yugoslavia | 0.346 | 0.886 | 0.874 |
| 19 | Romania | 0.290 | 0.834 | 0.864 |
| 20 | Iran | 0.272 | 0.838 | 0.853 |
| 21 | Syria | 0.261 | 0.751 | 0.867 |
| 22 | Colombia | 0.255 | 0.838 | 0.851 |
| 23 | Brazil | 0.246 | 0.818 | 0.850 |
| 24 | Korea | 0.206 | 0.821 | 0.842 |
| 25 | Malaysia | 0.190 | 0.854 | 0.823 |
| 26 | Thailand | 0.141 | 0.764 | 0.809 |
| 27 | Philippines | 0.140 | 0.758 | 0.817 |
| 28 | Sri Lanka | 0.103 | 0.776 | 0.800 |
| 29 | Pakistan | 0.089 | 0.732 | 0.783 |
| 30 | India | 0.068 | 0.758 | 0.770 |

## APPENDIX

Our starting point is the differential demand equation under preference independence,

$$w_i \mathrm{d}(\log q_i) = \theta_i \mathrm{d}(\log Q) + \phi\theta_i[\mathrm{d}(\log p_i) - \mathrm{d}(\log P^*)]$$

where $\mathrm{d}(\log Q) = \sum_i w_i\, \mathrm{d}(\log q_i)$ is the Divisia volume index and $\mathrm{d}(\log P^*) = \sum_i \theta_i \mathrm{d}(\log p_i)$ is the Frisch price index. It is easily verified that the covariance (2.1) can be written as the sum of two terms:

$$\mathrm{d}(\log Q) \sum_{i=1}^{n} w_i \left(\frac{\theta_i}{w_i} - 1\right)^2 + \phi \sum_{i=1}^{n} \theta_i[\mathrm{d}(\log p_i) - \mathrm{d}(\log P^*)]\frac{\theta_i}{w_i}$$

The first term is the real-income component of (2.1); it is equal to the real-income change multiplied by the Divisia variance of the income elasticities of the $n$ goods. The second term is the substitution component; it is a multiple $\phi$ of the Frisch covariance of the logarithmic price changes and the income elasticities.

Under Working's model the Divisia variance of the income elasticities can be written as the sum of $\beta_i^2/w_i$; in column 4 of Table 6-1 we specify $w_i$ as the arithmetic mean of $w_{ic}$ and $w_{i1}$ (1 = USA). Also, $\mathrm{d}(\log Q)$ is specified as the logarithmic difference between the values of country $c$ and the USA in column 13 of Table 1-6 of Theil et al. (1989).

We refer to Theil and Suhm (1981: Ch. 5) for a quality analysis based on pairs of countries, and to Theil (1976: Ch. 14) for the measurement of quality variations between and within groups of consumer goods.

## References

Cramer, J.S. (1973). "The interaction of income and price in consumer demand." *International Economic Review* 14: 351–363.

Frisch, R. (1959). "A complete scheme for computing all direct and cross demand elasticities in a model with many sectors." *Econometrica* 27: 177–196.

Hicks, J.R. and Allen, R.G.D. (1934). "A reconsideration of the theory of value." *Economica* New Series, 1: 52–76, 196–219.

Houthakker, H.S. (1952). "Compensated changes in quantities and qualities consumed." *Review of Economics Studies* 19: 155–164.

Theil, H. (1952). "Qualities, prices and budget enquiries." *Review of Economic Studies* 19: 129–147.

Theil, H. (1976). *Theory and Measurement of Consumer Demand.* Volume 2. Amsterdam: North-Holland Publishing Company.

Theil, H., Chung, C.-F. and Seale, J.L., Jr. (1989). *International Evidence on Consumption Patterns.* Greenwich, Conn.: JAI Press Inc.

Theil, H. and Suhm, F.E. (1981). *International Consumption Comparisons: A System-Wide Approach.* Amsterdam: North-Holland Publishing Company.

Von Neumann, J. and Morgenstern, O. (1947). *Theory of Games and Economic Behavior.* Second Edition. Princeton University Press.

CHAPTER 7

# A cross-country analysis of consumption patterns*

KENNETH W. CLEMENTS and HENRI THEIL

## 1. Introduction

Kravis and others (1978) made a detailed analysis of the components of the per capita gross domestic products of 16 countries. In this article we use the consumption components of their study for 1970 with four distinct objectives in mind. First, we want to verify Frisch's (1959: 189) conjecture according to which the income elasticity of the marginal utility of income takes negative values which increase algebraically toward zero as the consumer becomes more affluent. This conjecture was considered by several other authors, but the availability of consumption data for countries at quite different levels of affluence is a good reason for a reconsideration of this topic.

Second, we apply the differential approach to consumption theory in a cross-sectional context. Third, we measure the difference in the quality of consumption in different countries on the basis of the luxury-necessity distinction of the goods consumed. Fourth, we show how the differential approach can be combined with a partial specification of demand functions. The partial specification that will be considered is the Working (1943) – Leser (1963) model which expresses budget shares as linear functions of the logarithm of total expenditure. Let $p_i$ be the price and $q_i$ the quantity consumed of good $i$. Let $n$ be the number of goods so that $M = p_1q_1 + \ldots + p_nq_n$ is total expenditure (or income for short) and $w_i = p_iq_i/M$ is the budget share of good $i$. The Working-Leser model specifies

$$w_i = \alpha_i + \beta_i \log M \tag{1}$$

where $\alpha_i$ and $\beta_i$ are constants. This model represents an incomplete specification of demand functions because it contains no price substitution term, although it can be applied to the analysis of household budget data when all participating families pay the same price for each good. In Section 3 we shall

* Research supported in part by NSF Grant SOC76-82718. The authors are indebted to James Meisner for programming the computations and his helpful comments, and to Professor Robert Summers of the University of Pennsylvania for clarification of the data used in this paper.

show how the differential approach to consumption theory can be used to endow the Working-Leser model with a substitution term.

## 2. Estimation of the Working-Leser model

The application of the Working-Leser model to data for 16 countries requires that the 16 values of $M$ in (1) be expressed in the same unit. Kravis and his coauthors evaluated the quantities consumed in these different countries at the same "international" prices; these prices are obtained by weighting the prices of the participating countries in accordance with the size of larger regions which they are supposed to represent. Further details are beyond the scope of this paper; the result for total per capita consumption is shown in the first column of Table 7-1 with the value for India used as a base.[1] We shall use the figures in this column as real per capita incomes.

The data for 16 countries supplied by Kravis and his coauthors allow the use of 25 groups of consumer goods and services, but a much broader classification is appropriate for our objectives and is needed in order to give the assumption of identical tastes a chance of realism. Accordingly, we shall use four groups: food (including beverages and tobacco), clothing (including footwear), housing (rent, fuel, and home furnishings and operations), and the rest (all other goods and services). Scatter diagrams for these four goods indicate that (1) provides an excellent fit except for Kenya. The computations of this paper have been made both for all 16 countries including Kenya and for the 15 excluding Kenya. The results of the former computations were all less satisfactory than those of the latter. We have therefore decided to consider Kenya as a outlier; the discussion which follows is confined to the 15 countries listed in Table 7-1.

Estimates of the parameters $\alpha_i$ and $\beta_i$ of the model (1) can then be obtained from least-squares regressions of budget shares on the logarithm of the first column of Table 7-1. The estimates (with standard errors in parentheses) of the $\alpha_i$'s are for food 0.639 (0.023), clothing 0.075 (0.010), housing 0.111 (0.016), rest 0.174 (0.023). The estimates of the $\beta_i$'s are for food −0.171 (0.013), clothing, 0.006 (0.006), housing 0.054 (0.009), rest 0.111 (0.014). Thus, the $\beta_i$ of food is significantly negative, that of clothing is insignificant, and those of the two other groups are significantly positive. Also note that the $\alpha_i$'s have unit sum, while those of the $\beta_i$'s add up to zero; this is a direct consequence of the least-squares procedure.

[1] Total per capita consumption does not include line 110 of Kravis and others (1978), which concerns net expenditure of residents abroad; this is done in order to ensure consistency with the four components to be discussed in the next paragraph. The absence of Kenya from the table will also be discussed in the next paragraph. All data used in the paper are from Kravis and others (1978) Summary Multilateral Tables 4.1, p. 86 (per capita expenditures in local currencies) and 4.5, p. 96 (per capita quantities valued at international prices).

*Table 7-1.* Volume and quality of consumption and budget shares of food for 15 countries in 1970[a]

| | Per capita consumption | | | | | | | | | | | | | | | | |
|---|---|---|---|---|---|---|---|---|---|---|---|---|---|---|---|---|---|
| | Volume[b] | Quality[c] | India | Korea | Philippines | Malaysia | Colombia | Iran | Hungary | Italy | Japan | Netherlands | UK | Germany (W) | France | Belgium | U.S. |
| India | 1 | 1 | 639 | | | | | | | | | | | | | | |
| Korea | 1.78 | 1.04 | 590 | 541 | | | | | | | | | | | | | |
| Philippines | 1.90 | 1.06 | 584 | 535 | 530 | | | | | | | | | | | | |
| Malaysia | 2.57 | 1.11 | 559 | 509 | 504 | 478 | | | | | | | | | | | |
| Colombia | 2.64 | 1.12 | 556 | 507 | 502 | 476 | 474 | | | | | | | | | | |
| Iran | 2.76 | 1.12 | 552 | 503 | 497 | 472 | 469 | 465 | | | | | | | | | |
| Hungary | 5.76 | 1.19 | 490 | 440 | 435 | 409 | 407 | 403 | 340 | | | | | | | | |
| Italy | 6.77 | 1.15 | 476 | 427 | 421 | 395 | 393 | 389 | 326 | 312 | | | | | | | |
| Japan | 6.86 | 1.23 | 475 | 425 | 420 | 394 | 392 | 388 | 325 | 311 | 310 | | | | | | |
| Netherlands | 8.71 | 1.22 | 454 | 405 | 399 | 373 | 371 | 367 | 305 | 291 | 290 | 269 | | | | | |
| UK | 8.72 | 1.20 | 454 | 405 | 399 | 373 | 371 | 367 | 304 | 291 | 289 | 269 | 269 | | | | |
| Germany (W) | 9.01 | 1.27 | 451 | 402 | 396 | 371 | 368 | 364 | 302 | 288 | 287 | 266 | 266 | 263 | | | |
| France | 9.21 | 1.20 | 449 | 400 | 395 | 369 | 367 | 362 | 300 | 286 | 285 | 264 | 264 | 261 | 260 | | |
| Belgium | 9.68 | 1.24 | 445 | 396 | 390 | 364 | 362 | 358 | 296 | 282 | 281 | 260 | 260 | 257 | 255 | 251 | |
| U.S. | 13.84 | 1.31 | 415 | 365 | 360 | 334 | 332 | 328 | 265 | 251 | 250 | 230 | 229 | 227 | 225 | 221 | 190 |

[a] The budget shares of food in the last 15 columns of the table are to be divided by 1000.
[b] Sum of line numbers 1-109 in Summary Multilateral Table 4.5 of Kravis and others (1978), normalized so that India = 1.
[c] See Section 5.

To interpret the signs of the $\beta_i$'s we multiply (1) by $M$, which gives $p_iq_i = \alpha_iM + \beta_iM \log M$, and then differentiate with respect to $M$ (log = natural log),

$$\theta_i = \alpha_i + \beta_i (1 + \log M) \tag{2}$$

where $\theta_i = \partial(p_iq_i)/\partial M$ is the marginal share of good $i$. The ratio of the marginal share of a good to its budget share is equal to the income elasticity of this good: $\theta_i/w_i = \partial(\log q_i)/\partial(\log M)$. On combining (1) and (2) we then obtain

$$\frac{\theta_i}{w_i} = 1 + \frac{\beta_i}{w_i} \tag{3}$$

which shows that a good with positive (negative) $\beta_i$ has an income elasticity larger (smaller) than 1. The diagonal elements in the last 15 columns of Table 7-1 contain the budget shares of food that are implied by (1) and the $\alpha_i$ and $\beta_i$ estimates reported in the previous paragraph. The decline of this share for increasing per capita income agrees with Engel's law. The elements below the diagonal in these 15 columns will be explained in Section 4; the second column of Table 7-1 (which deals with the quality index) will be discussed in Section 5.

## 3. The substitution term and Frisch's conjecture

Our next step is the formulation of a substitution term for the Working-Leser model. For this purpose we proceed under the simplifying assumption that consumers are preference independent with respect to food, clothing, housing, and the rest. The differential demand equation for good $i$ can then be written in the form[2]

$$w_i\, \mathrm{d}(\log q_i) = \theta_i \mathrm{d}\left(\log \frac{M}{P}\right) + \phi\theta_i\, \mathrm{d}\left(\log \frac{p_i}{P'}\right) \tag{4}$$

where $\theta_i$ is (as before) the $i^{\text{th}}$ marginal share and the differentials of the logarithmic ratios on the right are to be interpreted as differences between differentials:

$$\mathrm{d}\left(\log \frac{M}{P}\right) = \mathrm{d}(\log M) - \mathrm{d}(\log P) \tag{5}$$

$$\mathrm{d}\left(\log \frac{p_i}{P'}\right) = \mathrm{d}(\log p_i) - \mathrm{d}(\log P') \tag{6}$$

[2] The general form of the differential demand system contains changes in all relative prices [see Theil (1980): Ch. 2)], but this is simplified to only one relative price change under preference independence, i.e., when the consumer's preferences can be represented by an additive utility function. Also, under preference independence all marginal shares are positive.

Here d(log $P$) is the Divisia price index in differential form,

$$d(\log P) = \sum_{i=1}^{n} w_i \, d(\log p_i) \tag{7}$$

and d(log $P'$) is the Frisch price index:

$$d(\log P') = \sum_{i=1}^{n} \theta_i \, d(\log p_i) \tag{8}$$

The first term on the right in (4) is the real-income component of the expression on the left, while the second right-hand term is the substitution component. The coefficient $\phi$ in the latter component is the reciprocal of the income elasticity of the marginal utility of income,

$$\phi = \left( \frac{\partial \log \lambda}{\partial \log M} \right)^{-1} \tag{9}$$

where $\lambda$ is the marginal utility of income. We shall refer to $\phi$ as the income flexibility.

Note the implication of (2) that the marginal shares are not constant under the Working-Leser model. In Section 4 we shall proceed conditionally on these marginal shares by substituting least-squares estimates for $\alpha_i$ and $\beta_i$ in (2). This means that $\phi$ is the only unknown in the differential demand system (4). As stated in Section 1, Frisch does not consider $\phi$ to be constant either; his conjecture on $1/\phi$ (the income elasticity of $\lambda$) is equivalent to a negative income flexibility $\phi$ which increases in absolute value when the consumer becomes more affluent. One way of verifying this conjecture is by multiplying (4) by the left-hand side of (6) and then summing over $i$. This yields

$$\sum_{i=1}^{n} w_i \, d(\log q_i) \, d\left( \log \frac{p_i}{P'} \right) = \phi \sum_{i=1}^{n} \theta_i \left[ d\left( \log \frac{p_i}{P'} \right) \right]^2 \tag{10}$$

where the real-income component disappears because $\theta_i$ d[log($p_i/P'$)] yields zero when summed over $i$. It follows from (6) that the sum on the right in (10) equals

$$\Pi' = \sum_{i=1}^{n} \theta_i [d(\log p_i) - d(\log P')]^2 \tag{11}$$

which is the Frisch variance of the logarithmic price displacements. Thus, we can derive $\phi$ by dividing the left side of (10) by $\Pi'$. This, basically, is the procedure that will be followed in the next section for the verification of Frisch's conjecture by means of the data on the 15 countries.[3]

[3] The method is similar to the efficient estimation procedure for $\phi$ under rational random behavior which is described by Theil (1975/6: Ch. 15) and applied by Clements and Theil (1978) and Theil and Clements (1978) to the demand for imports.

## 4. Verification of Frisch's conjecture

The standard application of differential demand systems is to time series data. The application (which has become known as the Rotterdam model) replaces infinitesimal logarithmic changes by finite log-changes from period $t - 1$ to period $t$ and the budget share $w_i$ by the arithmetic average value of $w_i$ in $t - 1$ and $t$. Here we are not concerned with changes over time but with cross-country data. To apply the differential approach to such data we shall consider a move from country $c$ to country $d$, where $c$ and $d$ take the values $1, \ldots, 15$ (the 15 countries listed in Table 7-1). In other words, whereas the time series application of the differential approach proceeds from one period to the next in a one-dimensional manner, the cross-section application to countries is two-dimensional and involves all pairs of countries. It must be admitted that the latter application considers moves, such as those from India to the U.S., which are a bit larger than the usual infinitesimal displacements of the differential approach. Nevertheless, it should be interesting to look at the results.

We proceed in the spirit of the Rotterdam model by using arithmetic average budget shares in the comparison of two countries $c$ and $d$. It follows from (1) that this amounts to

$$w_{icd} = \alpha_i + \beta_i \log \sqrt{Q_c Q_d} \tag{12}$$

where $Q_1, \ldots, Q_{15}$ are the numbers in the first column of Table 7-1.[4] For each good $i$ the matrix $[w_{icd}]$ is symmetric of order $15 \times 15$; the last 15 columns of Table 7-1 contain the diagonal elements of this matrix and those below the diagonal for $i$ = food, based on the estimates of $\alpha_i$ and $\beta_i$. A comparison of (1) and (2) shows that the corresponding marginal shares take the form

$$\theta_{icd} = \beta_i + w_{icd} \tag{13}$$

Therefore the matrix $[\theta_{icd}]$ for $i$ = food is obtained from the corresponding budget share matrix in Table 7-1 by subtracting 0.171 from each entry (the $\beta_i$ estimate for food being –0.171).

We define the finite-move version of the Frisch price-variance (11) from country $c$ to country $d$ as

$$\Pi'_{cd} = \sum_{i=1}^{n} \theta_{icd} \left( \log \frac{p_{id}}{p_{ic}} - P'_{cd} \right)^2 \tag{14}$$

where $p_{ic}$ is the price of good $i$ in country $c$ and

$$P'_{cd} = \sum_{i=1}^{n} \theta_{icd} \log \frac{p_{id}}{p_{ic}} \tag{15}$$

[4] We use Q's rather than M's in order to indicate that this column contains real rather than nominal incomes.

is the finite-move version of the Frisch price index from country $c$ to country $d$. Note that prices of individual goods can be expressed in local currency in (14); the effect of different currencies (of countries $c$ and $d$) is eliminated by the subtraction of $P'_{cd}$. The variance (14) is shown in Table 7-2 for each of the 105 country pairs. About one-half of the variances which compare the seven countries in Western Europe and North America are smaller than 0.01, whereas almost all other variances exceed 0.01. This means that there is comparatively little difference in the relative prices of the four goods (food, clothing, housing, and the rest) in the U.S. and the six countries of Western Europe.

The finite-move version of the left variable in (10) from country $c$ to country $d$ is similarly defined as

$$C_{cd} = \sum_{i=1}^{n} w_{icd} \log \frac{p_{id}}{p_{ic}} \left( \log \frac{p_{id}}{p_{ic}} - P'_{cd} \right) \tag{16}$$

where $w_{icd}$ is given in (12) and $q_{ic}$ is the per capita quantity of good $i$ consumed in country $c$. Recall from the end of Section 3 that $\phi$ equals the ratio of the left variable of (10) to the Frisch price variance. Accordingly, we define

$$\hat{\phi}_{cd} = \frac{C_{cd}}{\Pi'_{cd}} \tag{17}$$

as the estimate of $\phi$ based on the comparison of the consumption patterns of countries $c$ and $d$. These estimates for all 105 country pairs are shown in Table 7-3. The figures vary widely, but the vast majority (87 out of 105) have the correct negative sign. It is true that some estimates are far off, particularly the West German-Italian estimate which is positive and larger than 6, but this simply reflect a small difference in relative prices which prevents an accurate estimation of price substitution (see the West German-Italian Frisch price variance in Table 7-2, which is by far the smallest of all). The median of the 105 estimates of Tale 7-3 is –0.702, which is an entirely reasonable number.

To what extend do the estimates of Table 7-3 support Frisch's conjecture on the dependence of the income flexibility on the level of real income? Since the median of the 105 estimates is close to –0.7, one way of verifying this conjecture is the following. First, we consider the 15 estimates in the upper left part of Table 7-3, which are based on pairwise comparisons of the six poorest countries (from India to Iran). Six of these 15 estimates are algebraically smaller than –0.7. Second, we consider the next six countries by deleting India (with the smallest $Q_c$) and adding Hungary (the next in line after Iran). This yields another set of 15 estimates of $\phi$, five of which are algebraically smaller than –0.7. When we continue in this way by considering groups of successively richer countries, we should expect that the number of $\phi$ estimates algebraically smaller than –0.7 will increase if Frisch's conjecture is correct because this conjecture amounts to increasing $|\phi|$ with

*Table 7-2.* Frisch price variances for pairs of countries[a]

| | India | Korea | Philippines | Malaysia | Colombia | Iran | Hungary | Italy | Japan | Netherlands | U.K. | Germany (W) | France | Belgium |
|---|---|---|---|---|---|---|---|---|---|---|---|---|---|---|
| Korea | 157 | | | | | | | | | | | | | |
| Philippines | 210 | 91 | | | | | | | | | | | | |
| Malaysia | 1446 | 832 | 585 | | | | | | | | | | | |
| Colombia | 663 | 224 | 353 | 565 | | | | | | | | | | |
| Iran | 553 | 462 | 162 | 439 | 601 | | | | | | | | | |
| Hungary | 248 | 149 | 177 | 861 | 150 | 360 | | | | | | | | |
| Italy | 1002 | 653 | 401 | 239 | 370 | 168 | 384 | | | | | | | |
| Japan | 475 | 119 | 158 | 604 | 276 | 590 | 454 | 761 | | | | | | |
| Netherlands | 1587 | 1031 | 740 | 193 | 538 | 399 | 680 | 56 | 988 | | | | | |
| U.K. | 1005 | 451 | 346 | 162 | 154 | 364 | 363 | 157 | 324 | 200 | | | | |
| Germany (W) | 1164 | 710 | 492 | 231 | 323 | 274 | 402 | 15 | 746 | 36 | 115 | | | |
| France | 1602 | 1045 | 849 | 420 | 458 | 541 | 540 | 82 | 1058 | 54 | 236 | 38 | | |
| Belgium | 947 | 486 | 370 | 281 | 148 | 309 | 246 | 72 | 499 | 139 | 47 | 40 | 103 | |
| U.S. | 1764 | 1035 | 793 | 163 | 481 | 531 | 695 | 124 | 770 | 48 | 105 | 67 | 112 | 112 |

[a] All entries are to be divided by 10,000.

*Table 7-3.* Income flexibility estimates based on the pairs of countries

| | India | Korea | Philippines | Malaysia | Colombia | Iran | Hungary | Italy | Japan | Netherlands | U.K. | Germany (W) | France | Belgium |
|---|---|---|---|---|---|---|---|---|---|---|---|---|---|---|
| Korea | -1.21 | | | | | | | | | | | | | |
| Philippines | -0.64 | -0.85 | | | | | | | | | | | | |
| Malaysia | -0.21 | 0.00 | 0.12 | | | | | | | | | | | |
| Colombia | -0.10 | 0.29 | 0.19 | -0.21 | | | | | | | | | | |
| Iran | -1.15 | -1.53 | -1.40 | 0.03 | -0.98 | | | | | | | | | |
| Hungary | -0.44 | -0.70 | 0.27 | 0.06 | 0.63 | -1.54 | | | | | | | | |
| Italy | -0.92 | -0.97 | -0.81 | 0.50 | -0.57 | -2.31 | -0.96 | | | | | | | |
| Japan | -0.78 | -0.07 | -1.08 | 0.07 | -0.10 | -1.19 | -0.25 | -0.60 | | | | | | |
| Netherlands | -0.68 | -0.80 | -0.57 | -0.34 | -1.12 | -0.93 | -0.88 | 0.53 | -0.68 | | | | | |
| U.K. | -0.88 | -1.03 | -1.13 | 0.07 | -1.24 | -1.79 | -0.70 | 0.04 | -1.16 | -0.41 | | | | |
| Germany (W) | -0.51 | -0.76 | -0.22 | 0.26 | -1.33 | -0.54 | -0.84 | 6.42 | -0.67 | -0.87 | -0.63 | | | |
| France | -0.74 | -0.91 | -0.70 | -0.71 | -1.22 | -1.37 | -1.03 | -0.41 | -0.77 | -1.89 | -0.32 | -3.18 | | |
| Belgium | -0.76 | -1.08 | -0.78 | -0.12 | -1.65 | -1.66 | -0.91 | 0.60 | -1.03 | -0.57 | -0.92 | -1.00 | -0.19 | |
| U.S. | -0.51 | -0.59 | -0.49 | -1.13 | -0.97 | -1.01 | -0.60 | 0.49 | -0.69 | -0.88 | 0.12 | -1.21 | -0.24 | -0.19 |

increasing real income [see the discussion preceding eq. (10)]. The number of these $\phi$ estimates for the successive country groups is 6 (India to Iran), 5 (Korea to Hungary), 6, 5, 8, 8, 5, 5, 8, 7 (Netherlands to U.S.). These numbers do not reveal much of a monotone increase that would confirm Frisch's conjecture. We shall have more to say about this matter at the end of Section 5, which is concerned with the quality differentials of the consumption patterns in the 15 countries.

## 5. An international quality comparison

We introduced Divisia and Frisch price indexes in Section 3. The corresponding volume indexes are

$$d(\log Q) = \sum_{i=1}^{n} w_i \, d(\log q_i) \tag{18}$$

$$d(\log Q') = \sum_{i=1}^{n} \theta_i \, d(\log q_i) \tag{19}$$

Subtraction of (18) from (19) yields

$$d\left(\log \frac{Q'}{Q}\right) = \sum_{i=1}^{n} w_i \left(\frac{\theta_i}{w_i} - 1\right) d(\log q_i) \tag{20}$$

where the left side, similarly to (5), should be interpreted as the difference between $d(\log Q')$ and $d(\log Q)$.

Since the income elasticities $\theta_1/w_1, \ldots, \theta_n/w_n$ have a unitary Divisia mean, i.e., $\sum_i w_i(\theta_i/w_i) = \sum_i \theta_i = 1$, the right side of (20) is the Divisia covariance of the income elasticities and the logarithmic quantity changes of the $n$ goods. This covariance is positive (negative) when the composition of the consumer's basket changes so that the quantities of luxuries increase (decrease) on the average relative to those of necessities. The consumer considers luxuries more attractive than necessities because an increase in his income, prices remaining constant, induces him to allocate a larger proportion of his income to luxuries and a smaller proportion to necessities. He will buy more high-priced coffee with a large income elasticity and less low-priced coffee with a small income elasticity. Thus, a positive (negative) sign of the Divisia covariance in (20) indicates that the composition of the consumer's basket has become more (less) attractive from his point of view, which we shall express by referring to the left side of (20) as the quality index of the consumer's basket in differential form.[5]

Expressing this quality change in terms of income and price changes is a matter of substituting demand equations for quantity changes. When we use the differential demand system (4) under preference independence, we obtain

[5] See also Chapter 6.

the following result after minor rearrangements:

$$d\left(\log\frac{Q'}{Q}\right) = d\left(\log\frac{M}{P}\right)\sum_{i=1}^{n} w_i\left(\frac{\theta_i}{w_i}-1\right)^2 + \phi\sum_{i=1}^{n}\theta_i\, d\left(\log\frac{p_i}{P'}\right)\frac{\theta_i}{w_i} \tag{21}$$

The first term on the right is the real-income component of the change in quality; this term is equal to the logarithmic change in real income multiplied by the Divisia variance of the income elasticities of the *n* goods, which means that this variance can be viewed as the income elasticity of the demand for quality.[6] The last term in (21) is the substitution component of the quality change; it is equal to a multiple $\phi$ of the Frisch (not Divisia!) covariance of the logarithmic price changes and the income elasticities of the *n* goods. This covariance is positive when the prices of luxuries increase relative to those of necessities. Therefore, given the negative sign of $\phi$, the substitution component of the quality change is then negative as we would expect it to be.

We now return to the Working-Leser model and note that (3) simplified (20) to

$$d\left(\log\frac{Q'}{Q}\right) = \sum_{i=1}^{n}\beta_i\, d(\log q_i) \tag{22}$$

Since the $\beta_i$'s are constants, the quality index of the Working-Leser model can thus be written in level form as $\prod_i q_i^{\beta_i}$. This index is shown in the second column in Table 7-1 for the 15 countries based on the estimates of the $\beta_i$'s of the four goods, with India used as base. The results show a strong positive association between the quality index and the real-income index in the first column, which is not really surprising.

We proceed to consider the finite-move version of (21) from country *c* to country *d* under the Working-Leser model. For the left variable we obtain, using (22),

$$\sum_{i=1}^{n}\beta_i\log\frac{q_{id}}{q_{ic}} \tag{23}$$

We conclude from (21) that the real-income component of the quality difference (23) is equal to log $(Q_d/Q_c)$ multiplied by the Divisia variance of the income elasticities, where $Q_1, \ldots, Q_{15}$ are the figures in the first column of Table 7-1. It follows from (3) that under the Working-Leser model this variance equals $V = \sum_i w_i(\beta_i/w_i)^2 = \sum_i \beta_i^2/w_i$, so that (1) yields[7]

$$V = \sum_{i=1}^{n}\frac{\beta_i^2}{\alpha_i + \beta_i\log M} \tag{24}$$

[6] It is easily shown that d[log $(M/P)$] is identical to the Divisia volume index (18).

[7] The derivative of $V$ in (24) with respect to log $M$ is equal to minus the third-order Divisia moment of the income elasticities of the *n* goods around their Divisia mean (which is 1). Since

For the finite-move version (23) we define the real-income component as $V_{cd} \log (Q_d/Q_c)$, where

$$V_{cd} = \sum_{i=1}^{n} \frac{\beta_i^2}{\alpha_i + \beta_i \log \sqrt{Q_c Q_d}} \tag{25}$$

Therefore, the quality difference between the consumption patterns of countries $c$ and $d$ corrected for the effect of real income is

$$\sum_{i=1}^{n} \beta_i \log \frac{q_{id}}{q_{ic}} - V_{cd} \log \frac{Q_d}{Q_c} \tag{26}$$

Before proceeding to the substitution component of (23) we should consider the problem of how to measure the extent to which the differences in real income account for the observed quality differences. One way of doing this is by means of sums of squares. The expression to be explained is then the sum of the squares of (23),

$$\sum_{c=1}^{15} \sum_{d=1}^{15} \left( \sum_{i=1}^{n} \beta_i \log \frac{q_{id}}{q_{ic}} \right)^2$$

which gives 2.545 when least-squares estimates are substituted for the $\beta_i$'s. The analogous sum of squares of (26) equals 0.497, which shows that the real-income differences among the 15 countries account for a little over 80 percent of the observed pairwise quality differences.

Finally, we consider the contribution of price substitution to the explanation of these quality differences. We write the finite-move version from country $c$ to country $d$ of the substitution term in (21) as $\phi S_{cd}$, where

$$S_{cd} = \sum_{i=1}^{n} \theta_{icd} \left( \log \frac{p_{id}}{p_{ic}} - P'_{cd} \right) \frac{\theta_{icd}}{w_{icd}} \tag{27}$$

with $\theta_{icd}$, $P'_{cd}$, and $w_{icd}$ defined in (12) to (15). Thus, by subtracting $\phi S_{cd}$ from (26) we obtain the residual component of the quality difference (23). So we consider

$$F(\phi) = \sum_{c=1}^{15} \sum_{d=1}^{15} \left( \sum_{i=1}^{n} \beta_i \log \frac{q_{id}}{q_{ic}} - V_{cd} \log \frac{Q_d}{Q_c} - \phi S_{cd} \right)^2 \tag{28}$$

which is the residual sum of squares over all country pairs as a function of $\phi$. This function is quadratic with a minimum at $\phi = -0.678$, which is in satisfactory agreement with the median $-0.702$ of the $\phi$ estimates of Table 7-3. The minimum value of the function (28) is 0.305. On comparing this with the number 0.497 reported in the previous paragraph, we conclude that

---

$V$ equals the income elasticity of the demand for quality, the effect of an income change on this elasticity under the Working-Leser model thus depends on the skewness of the Divisia-weighted distribution of the income elasticities of the $n$ goods.

price substitution accounts for a fraction (0.192)/(0.497) or almost 40 percent of the observed pairwise quality differences after these are corrected for the effect of real-income differences. The joint contribution of the differences in real income and relative prices to the explanation of the pairwise quality differences is about 88 percent.

The procedure of minimizing (28) wit respect to $\phi$ implies the use of a $\phi$ which is independent of the level of real income. We concluded at the end of Section 4 that the $\phi$ estimates of Table 7-3 provide little support for such a dependence. Frisch was correct in emphasizing the importance of the income flexibility for the measurement of price substitution, particularly under preference independence, but his suggestions on the dependence of the flexibility on the level of real income cannot be easily supported by data. Since $1/\phi$ is the income elasticity of the marginal utility of income, the dependence of $\phi$ on the level of real income has the nature of a third-order derivative of utility with respect to income. Statistical data are usually not cooperative in conveying information on derivatives of such high order. The 88 percent contribution of real income and relative prices to the explanation of quality differences which we reported in the previous paragraph is quite satisfactory. Making $\phi$ dependent on the level of real income may score a few extra percentage points, but it should be doubted whether such a refinement is worthwhile, given the strong assumptions of preference independence and identical tastes across consumers of different countries. Also, the numerical value of about –0.7 for $\phi$ is of the same order as that obtained by others. We refer to Biørn (1974), De Janvry and others (1972), Lluch and others (1977: 74–81), Paulus (1972), Theil (1975/6, Section 15.4), Theil and Brooks (1971), and Van Praag (1971) for various theoretical and empirical results on this matter.

## References

Biørn, E. (1974). "Estimating the flexibility of the marginal utility of income." *European Economic Review* 5: 177–185.

Clements, K.W. and Theil, H. (1978). "A simple method of estimating price elasticities in international trade." *Economics Letters* 1: 133–137.

De Janvry, A., Biery, J. and Nuñez, A. (1972). "Estimation of demand parameters under consumer budgeting: An application to Argentina." *American Journal of Agricultural Economics* 54: 422–430.

Frisch, R. (1959). "A complete scheme for computing all direct and cross demand elasticities in a model with many sectors." *Econometrica* 27: 177–196.

Kravis, I.B., Heston, A.W. and Summers, R. (1978). *International Comparisons of Real Product and Purchasing Power*. Baltimore, Md.: The Johns Hopkins University Press.

Leser, C.E.V. (1963). "Forms of Engel functions." *Econometrica* 31: 694–703.

Lluch, C., Powell, A.A. and Williams, R.A. (1977). *Patterns in Household Demand and Saving*. Oxford University Press.

Paulus, J.D. (1972). *The Estimation of Large Systems of Consumer Demand Equations Using Stochastic Prior Information*. Doctoral dissertation, The University of Chicago.

Theil, H. (1975/76). *Theory and Measurement of Consumer Demand*. Two volumes. Amsterdam: North-Holland Publishing Company.

Theil, H. (1980). *The System-Wide Approach to Microeconomics.* The University of Chicago Press.

Theil, H. and Brooks, R.B. (1971). "How does the marginal utility of income change when real income changes?" *European Economic Review* 2: 218–240.

Theil, H. and Clements, K.W. (1978). "A differential approach to U.S. import demand." *Economics Letters* 1: 249–252.

Van Praag, B. (1971). "The welfare function in Belgium: An empirical investigation." *European Economic Review* 2: 337–369.

Working, H. (1943). "Statistical laws of family expenditure." *Journal of the American Statistical Association* 38: 43–56.

# Name index

## Advanced Studies in Theoretical and Applied Econometrics

1. J.H.P. Paelinck (ed.): *Qualitative and Quantitative Mathematical Economics.* 1982 ISBN 90-247-2623-9
2. J.P. Ancot (ed.): *Analysing the Structure of Econometric Models.* 1984 ISBN 90-247-2894-0
3. A.J. Hughes Hallet (ed.): *Applied Decision Analysis and Economic Behaviour.* 1984 ISBN 90-247-2968-8
4. J.K. Sengupta: *Information and Efficiency in Economic Decision.* 1985 ISBN 90-247-3072-4
5. P. Artus and O. Guvenen (eds.), in collaboration with F. Gagey: *International Macroeconomic Modelling for Policy Decisions.* 1986 ISBN 90-247-3201-8
6. M.J. Vilares: *Structural Change in Macroeconomic Models.* Theory and Estimation. 1986 ISBN 90-247-3277-8
7. C. Carraro and D. Sartore (eds.): *Development of Control Theory for Economic Analysis.* 1987 ISBN 90-247-3345-6
8. D.P. Broer: *Neoclassical Theory and Empirical Models of Aggregate Firm Behaviour.* 1987 ISBN 90-247-3412-6
9. A. Italianer: *Theory and Practice of International Trade Linkage Models.* 1986 ISBN 90-247-3407-X
10. D.A. Kendrick: *Feedback.* A New Framework for Macroeconomic Policy. 1988 ISBN 90-247-3593-9; Pb: 90-247-3650-1
11. J.K. Sengupta and G.K. Kadekodi (eds.): *Econometrics of Planning and Efficiency.* 1988 ISBN 90-247-3602-1
12. D.A. Griffith: *Advanced Spatial Statistics.* Special Topics in the Exploration of Quantitative Spatial Data Series. 1988 ISBN 90-247-3627-7
13. O. Guvenen (ed.): *International Commodity Market Models and Policy Analysis.* 1988 ISBN 90-247-3768-0
14. G. Arbia: *Spatial Data Configuration in Statistical Analysis of Regional Economic and Related Problems.* 1989 ISBN 0-7923-0284-2
15. B. Raj (ed.): *Advances in Econometrics and Modelling.* 1989 ISBN 0-7923-0299-0
16. A. Aznar Grasa: *Econometric Model Selection.* A New Approach. 1989 ISBN 0-7923-0321-0
17. L.R. Klein and J. Marquez (eds.): *Economics in Theory and Practice.* An Eclectic Approach. Essays in Honor of F. G. Adams. 1989 ISBN 0-7923-0410-1
18. D.A. Kendrick: *Models for Analyzing Comparative Advantage.* 1990 ISBN 0-7923-0528-0
19. P. Artus and Y. Barroux (eds.): *Monetary Policy.* A Theoretical and Econometric Approach. 1990 ISBN 0-7923-0626-0

## Advanced Studies in Theoretical and Applied Econometrics

20. G. Duru and J.H.P. Paelinck (eds.): *Econometrics of Health Care.* 1990
ISBN 0-7923-0766-6
21. L. Phlips (ed.): *Commodity, Futures and Financial Markets.* 1991
ISBN 0-7923-1043-8
22. H.M. Amman, D.A. Belsley and L.F. Pau (eds.): *Computational Economics and Econometrics.* 1992 ISBN 0-7923-1287-2
23. B. Raj and J. Koerts (eds.): *Henri Theil's Contributions to Economics and Econometrics.* Vol. I: Econometric Theory and Methodology. 1992
ISBN 0-7923-1548-0
24. B. Raj and J. Koerts (eds.): *Henri Theil's Contributions to Economics and Econometrics.* Vol. II: Consumer Demand Analysis and Information Theory. 1992
ISBN 0-7923-1664-9
25. B. Raj and J. Koerts (eds.): *Henri Theil's Contributions to Economics and Econometrics.* Vol. III: Economic Policy and Forecasts, and Management Science. 1992 ISBN 0-7923-1665-7
Set (23-25) ISBN 0-7923-1666-5
26. P. Fisher: *Rational Expectations in Macroeconomic Models.* 1992
ISBN 0-7923-1903-6
27. L. Phlips and L.D. Taylor (eds.): *Aggregation, Consumption and Trade.* Essays in Honor of H.S. Houthakker. 1992. ISBN 0-7923-2001-8
28. L. Mátyás and P. Sevestre (eds.): *The Econometrics of Panel Data.* Handbook of Theory and Applications. 1992 ISBN 0-7923-2043-3
29. S. Selvanathan: *A System-Wide Analysis of International Consumption Patterns.* 1993 ISBN 0-7923-2344-0
30. H. Theil in association with D. Chen, K. Clements and C. Moss: *Studies in Global Econometrics.* 1996 ISBN 0-7923-3660-7
31. P.J. Kehoe and T.J. Kehoe (eds.): *Modeling North American Economic Integration.* 1995 ISBN 0-7923-3751-4
32. C. Wells: *The Kalman Filter in Finance.* 1996 ISBN 0-7923-3771-9

**Kluwer Academic Publishers – Dordrecht / Boston / London**

**Batch number: 10816040**

Printed by Printforce, the Netherlands